Alex Athanassakos

In Pursuit of Economic Growth and Large Families

Toronto, 2019

Alex Athanassakos was born in Greece in 1952 and migrated to Toronto, Canada in 1978 where he presently lives. He obtained his Ph.D. in Economics from York University in 1982. He published his first book, "*Our Travels with Alexander-Taking a year off in France*", on Amazon in 2014, and his second, "*On Democracy - A Novel*", in July 2015.

Table of Contents

Introduction 1
Fairness, Equality & Democracy 3
Population 5
    Summary 5
    The Past 6
    The Future 9
    Inequality 15
    Malthus 18
Consumption 23
    Summary 23
    The Past 23
    The Future 25
Impacts 31
    Summary 31
    Greenhouse Gas Emissions – aka Climate Change 32
        Loss of biodiversity and food sources 37
        Extreme Weather 41
        Sea Level Rise 52
        Summary of impacts of climate change 54
    Water 56
        Water Quantity 56
        Water Quality 58
    Air Quality 62
    Summary of Impacts 64
    Food 65
Conclusion 69
Appendix A 81
    Fairness vs. Equality 81
    Direct vs. Representative Democracy 93

< Introduction >

"Another such victory over the Romans and we are undone."
— King Pyrrhus of Epirus in the Battle of Asculum, his second Pyrrhic Victory against the Romans, 279 BC

On any objective measure, people today (by no means all people) have it better than they did 100 years ago: life expectancy is up, real per capita consumption is up, infant mortality is down, the number of major wars is down, literacy is up, caloric intake is up, slavery is (in principle) abolished, women can now vote and participate, if they so choose, in the labour force (by no means in all countries), and so on. Should economic equality also be part of the benchmarks we use to measure progress? This is the first question this book is going to address.

For some people, the answer is an unequivocal "No". For them, the means of achieving a goal are more important than the goal itself. For example, we could improve many people's economic status by killing all the billionaires, stealing their money, and re-distributing it to those in need. But for most people, this would constitute an abhorrent process for achieving economic equality. This group, implicitly, or explicitly, accepts merit, inheritance (both biological and economic), good luck, effort and "playing by the rules" as sacrosanct and leaves questions of income redistribution up to an individual's choice. But why should good luck and inheritance be sacrosanct? Who decided that this is so? And who set the rules that define the play?

For other people, the answer is also unequivocal, but this time it is a "Yes". Presumably, these people's stance emanates from feelings of compassion towards the economically underprivileged. But is that all there is or is there also a feeling of jealousy – "if I don't have a Porsche, no-one should"? And what about the means of getting there? In a world where a wealth distribution already exists, achieving equality may involve treating many people unfairly. Why then should our feelings of compassion extend only to end states and not to the process of getting there?

And yet for others, whatever approach their "holy" books prescribe is the acceptable one – i.e., their God tells them what to accept.

But, if we live in a democratic society by choice, then answers to such questions should reflect the Will of the majority. In this case, then, would a majority vote for economic equality given the chance? And if they did, would it be feasible to achieve it?

The second question this book is going to address is this: because we have made progress, relative to the benchmarks mentioned above, does this mean that this progress will continue forever? Is there a point in time when we can no longer afford the costs of our progress? Is economic growth enough to compensate us for the loss of other qualitative aspects of life? For example, the pleasure lost when unable to swim in any body of water without fear of infection; the sadness experienced in knowing that there are no more white rhinoceroses roaming in Africa; the inability to smell the roses in the gasoline-infused air of today's cities; the loss of "tomatines" in tomatoes engineered for size, rather than flavor, because there are so many of us to feed? Are population and economic growth "weapons of mass destruction" that will eventually make everyone worse off through their environmental impacts?

Finally, since many of today's environmental problems require political solutions at the global level (environmental problems seldomly stay local), what form of political organization is best suited to avoid lose-lose scenarios with respect to our unrelenting pursuit of progress?

A note on data: Our international organizations, such as the United Nations and its numerous sub-agencies, the World Bank, and the IMF, need to do a better job collecting and presenting data. At present, data collection appears haphazard and relies mainly on the member states to do it. But we know that for most states in the world, data collection is the last thing on their mind, either because of lack of resources and expertise or because of political agendas. As such, the priority for our international organizations should be to collect quality data rather than developing arbitrary policies and programs. Without data, policy is bound to fail.

< Fairness, Equality & Democracy >

*"Democracy is a device that ensures we shall be governed
no better than we deserve."*
— George Bernard Shaw (1856-1950)

Since a full discussion on fairness and democracy is peripheral to the main themes of this book, I have moved such discussion to Appendix A. Here it may suffice to state the following summary of it:

1. Studies have found that people have a favorable bias towards fairness rather than economic equality. And when there is a clash between fairness and equality, people seem to prefer a fair inequality to an unfair equality. And this result seems to hold across the political spectrum, as well as across demographics, and countries.

2. Fairness is not about outcomes but rather about the process and circumstances that led to those outcomes. The fairness of any outcome cannot be evaluated without reference to the rules that generated it. As such, if the rules that generate an outcome are fair, then the outcome is also fair.

3. It follows then from item 2 above, that fairness is not a unique and universal concept or rule that holds true irrespective of circumstances. Rather, it is a contextual concept or rule. It is also not an objective "thing" that exists out there independently of us. Rather, in a democracy, it is what the majority deems it to be.

4. In a democracy, the existence of individual rights, as well as any conditions on them, depends on the wishes of the majority – in theory. Although it is true that in representative democracies individual rights, and any restrictions on them, depend on the wishes of the people's representatives and their sponsors, it is nevertheless also true that in the long-run these wishes cannot diverge too far from those of the majority (e.g., slavery, women's suffrage, apartheid, freedom of expression, equality before the law, etc.) – you may justifiably wonder at this point how long the long-run is.

5. Since the exercise of any human right may interfere with the rights of other people, when the costs of interference become too high the only way to resolve the ensuing conflicts is through majority voting.

As such, the only right that is (or should be) unconditional in a democracy is the right to vote and the right of the majority to impose its Will.

6. Elected governments in most representative democracies are seldomly supported by a majority of voters. This is the case in the first-past-the post and the Electoral College systems, but it is also true in democracies with proportional representation when the winner is unable to get a majority of seats and is therefore forced to form a coalition government without any further appeal to the voters.

7. Representative democracies are by their nature susceptible to corruption and favorably pre-disposed towards implementing policies that benefit the few who pull the strings of the people's representatives. As such, if we want solutions to our present problems, we will need to move away from the representative democracy model and closer to a direct democracy model.

At this point you may be wondering how a discussion on fairness, human rights and democracy relates to the book's title – that is how does it relate to economic growth and large families? The answer is simple: if most of our current problems – climate change, air pollution, extermination of other species, deforestation, pollution of fresh and oceanic water, local conflicts, migrations, etc. – are consequences of more and more people living and consuming on this planet, then the question could be asked as to whether or not it is fair to respect one's desire for a large family, or a second car, to the detriment of everyone else. Freedom of choice, after all, is not an unlimited right. One could exercise one's freedom any way one wants, provided that this does not interfere with the rights of other people – like their right not to die from air pollution (as we will see later, "life, liberty and the pursuit of happiness" are all under threat by climate change). Otherwise, the person whose "freedom" takes precedence over all other people's freedoms is a dictator – an outcome not very desirable in a democracy.

But, before we make childbearing, or private consumption, a public issue, and make it subject to majority vote, we must be certain that most of our problems today and in the future (especially in the future), are the result of more and more people living and consuming on this planet, right? So, let us have a look.

< Population[1] >

"Anyone who believes in indefinite growth of anything physical on a physically finite planet is either a madman or an economist."
— Kenneth Boulding, economist (1910-1993)

Summary

This is a summary of what the population data tell us:

1. The countries that contributed the most to the increase in the world's population over the last 67 years were all poor, except for the United States, and were mainly located in Asia.

2. The countries that will contribute the most to the increase in the world's population over the next 32 years are all poor and located mainly in Africa.

3. The higher a country's population and the higher its growth rate, the poorer the country.

4. Poverty and high population growth lead to more poverty which leads to local conflicts and to migration.

5. For a receiving country, immigration is good only if the country has a labour shortage relative to its resources, and further if it can choose which immigrants to accept.

6. In many poor countries with high population growth having children does not appear to be beneficial to themselves, to their compatriots, or to their neighbours.

7. The biological "instinct" for having children does not appear to be very strong as birth rates have been in continuous decline due to other choice factors, such as the choice to use birth control, or the choice to pursue a career.

---

[1] All population data come from United Nations, Population Division, Department of Economic and Social Affairs, 2017 revision.

The Past

Over the last 67 years, the world's population increased at an average annual rate of 1.64%. By 2017, it had tripled in size, compared to 1950. But, although the world's population increased in absolute numbers, its rate of growth decreased. In other words, the world's population is getting bigger, but at a slower and slower rate – from 1.87% in 1951 to 1.16% in 2017.

At the risk of sounding tautological, the population of the world increases only when new babies are born. This is not necessarily so at the country level where the population could increase, or decrease, through migration. Population counts at the country level are based on the de facto population of a country which includes all residents regardless of legal status – except for unprocessed refugees; these are counted in their home countries.

In 1951 the world's population increased by 1.87% over the previous year, which means that only 3.74% of the people had children, accidentally or on purpose – it takes two to have a child. This proportion had fallen to 2.32% in 2017 – a 38% reduction. This reduction could be the result of better and cheaper birth controls, which allowed people to have sex without accidents, as well as the result of prioritizing other things in life over children – as opposed to the reasons provided in the TV series "The Handmaid's Tale".

Is the average rate of growth of the world's population applicable to all countries? No. The United Arab Emirates experienced the highest growth rate between 1950 and 2017 (13,480%), followed by Qatar (10,456%), Western Sahara (3,914%), Kuwait (2,602%), Sint Maarten (2,576%) Jordan (1,916%), Mayotte (1,571%), Djibouti (1,443%), Bahrain (1,191%) and Andorra (1,142%) – see Table 1.

Did all countries experience growth? No. Six countries, accounting for 0.1% of the world's population in 2015, experienced declines since 1950, and ten experienced declines since 1960 (Table 2). These declines do not necessarily mean that the birth rates in those countries collapsed. As we mentioned, migration could reduce, or increase a country's population. This is more evident in the case of the Holy See which in theory should have zero births – we hope, but then who knows what really happens within the Vatican walls.

The countries that contributed the most to the increase in the world's population between 1950 and 2017, were India (963 million) and China (855 million). These two countries, along with the other eight shown in Table 4, accounted for 59% of the increase in the world's population – India's increase was three times the size of the entire population of the United States in 2017!

Table 1: Countries with the Highest Population Growth 1950 – 2017

Country	Population 1950 (Millions)	Population 2017 (Millions)	% Change 2017/50	GDP per capita 2017 PPP*
UAE	0.70	9.40	13,408%	$68,200
Qatar	0.03	2.64	10,456%	$124,900
W. Sahara	0.01	0.55	3,914%	$2,500
Kuwait	0.15	4.14	2,602%	$69,700
Sint Maarten	0.001	0.04	2,576%	$66,800
Jordan	0.48	9.7	1,916%	$12,500
Mayotte	0.015	0.25	1,571%	$4,900
Djibouti	0.062	0.96	1,443%	$3,600
Bahrain	0.12	1.58	1,191%	$51,800
Andorra	0.006	0.077	1,142%	$49,900
World	2,536	7,550	198%	$23,350

Source: United Nations, Population Division, Department of Economic and Social Affairs, 2017 revision; CIA, the World Factbook. *PPP= Purchasing Power Parity. It measures how much the same basket of goods and services costs relative to a base country's currency, in this case, the US dollar.

The countries with the highest growth rates were all (and still are) extremely small – the smallest in 1950 was Sint Maarten (1,499) and the largest was Jordan (481,321). As such, if these countries had any hopes of developing their economies, then they had to increase their population base.

Table 2: Countries with declining populations

Countries	Population In 2015	% Rate of change 2015/1950	% Rate of change 2015/1960
Saint Helena	4,034	-18.9%	-15.0%
Georgia	3,951,524	12.0%	-1.4%
Bulgaria	7,177,396	-1.0%	-9.0%
Hungary	9,783,925	4.8%	-2.2%
Latvia	1,992,663	3.4%	-6.4%
Holy See	803	-11.6%	-11.4%
Montserrat	5,124	-62.1%	-57.7%
Cook Islands	17,449	15.7%	4.4%
Niue	1,629	-65.1%	66.2%
Tokelau	1,252	-20.1%	33.2%

Source: United Nations, Population Division, Department of Economic and Social Affairs, 2017 revision

Given how well the countries in Table 1 did in growing their populations, did they also do as well in growing their economies? Well, six of them did very well, but four did not. Andorra, Sint Maarten and the four countries from the Arabian Peninsula achieved a per capita GDP much higher than the world's average - in fact, in 2017 Qatar had the second highest per capita income after Lichtenstein and double that of the United States. Unfortunately, data on the distribution of income in these countries either do not exist, or they do but for only a few recent years. As such, we cannot tell whether all the residents in those countries did equally well. But the two African countries and Jordan achieved a per capita GDP much lower than the world's average (Table 1).

What would explain the differences in the GDP per capita among these countries? The main difference is that the population of the Arab countries increased as part of a plan to acquire the labour needed for development. But for the others, no such plan was in place.

As Table 3 shows, all the oil producing countries in the Arabian Peninsula have populations that consist, in large part, of immigrants (37% for Saudi Arabia at the low end and 88% for UAE at the high end). This means that the population growth among the Arab countries was not the result of more indigenous babies being born, but rather the result of importing labour primarily from India, but also from Pakistan. Even if the increase in the absolute numbers of UAE's population was large, relative to the world's, UAE would not have counted as a major contributor to the world's population growth because its growth was the result of shifting people across countries rather than giving birth to new humans.

Table 3: Stock of Migrants	
In:	As a % of its total population in 2017
Bahrain	48%
Jordan	33%
Kuwait	76%
Oman	45%
Qatar	65%
Saudi Arabia	37%
United Arab Emirates	88%
Andorra	53%
Western Sahara	1%
Mayotte	29%
Djibouti	12%
Source: UN, Department of Economic and Social Affairs. Population Division. Trends in International Migrant Stock: The 2017 revision	

For Jordan, on the other hand, the increase was mainly due to the displacement of Palestinians after their conflict with Israel. For Western Sahara, the first burst in population growth (14%) occurred in 1976, the year when Spain transferred the administration of the region to Morocco and Mauritania. As such, its population growth could be the result of territorial reconfiguration or movement of people from Morocco and Mauritania (that's why the share of its population that consists of migrants is very low). Finally, for Djibouti, its growth rates peaked between 1974 and 1979 which coincides with the independence of Djibouti from France (1977) and the ensuing influx of mainly Somali immigrants who were escaping the 1976 communist dictatorship, the ensuing war in 1977 and 1978 and the civil war in 1991.

Immigration then is good for a country's economy if that country has a very limited labour force, if it has resources to exploit that are in high demand worldwide, and if it can choose the kind of immigrants that it will accept. All of these conditions were true for the Arab countries, but not true for Jordan, Western Sahara, and Djibouti.

Table 4: Countries with the largest absolute change in population

Country	Population 2017 (Millions)	Absolute increase 2017/1950 (Millions)	% Rate of change in population 2017/1950	GDP per capita PPP, 2017
India	1,339	963	256%	$7,200
China	1,410	855	154%	$17,000
Indonesia	264	194	280%	$12,400
USA	324	166	104%	$59,500
Pakistan	197	159	425%	$5,400
Brazil	209	155	288%	$15,500
Nigeria	191	153	404%	$5,900
Bangladesh	165	127	335%	$4,200
Mexico	129	101	361%	$19,500
Ethiopia	105	87	479%	$2,100
World	7,550	5,014	198%	$23,350

Source: United Nations, Population Division, Department of Economic and Social Affairs, 2017 revision; CIA, the World Factbook

But enough about the countries with the highest growth rates. How about the ones with the largest absolute increases in population? The ten countries that contributed the most to the increase in the world's population are all, except for the US, poor with an average per capita income much lower than the world's average (Table 4). A cursory glance at Table 4 reveals that for large countries, the larger the population and the larger its growth rate, the lower the per capita GDP.

The Future

What about the future? According to the UN, although the annual growth rate of the world's population will continue to decline (0.53% by 2050), our planet will have 9.8 billion souls living on it in 2050. Niger will grow the most between 2017 and 2050 (219%), followed by nine other countries all from Africa (Table 5).

Country	Population 2017	% Rate of Change 2017-2050	GDP Per Capita (in PPP)
Niger	21,477,348	218.7%	$5,900
Angola	29,784,193	155.3%	$6,800
Uganda	42,862,958	146.6%	$2,400
Somalia	14,742,523	143.2%	$400
D. R. Congo	81,339,988	142.7%	$800
Tanzania	57,310,019	140.9%	$3,300
Zambia	17,094,130	139.9%	$4,000
Mali	18,541,980	137.4%	$2,200
Burundi	10,864,245	137.1%	$800
Mozambique	29,668,834	128.4%	$1,300

Table 5: The countries with the highest population growth 2017-2050

Source: United Nations, Population Division, Department of Economic and Social Affairs, 2017 revision; CIA, the World Factbook

As for the top countries with the largest increases in absolute numbers, the US, Pakistan, and India are still there, but all the other countries are now African countries. These ten countries will account for 52% of the 2.2 billion increase in the world's population (see the graph below).

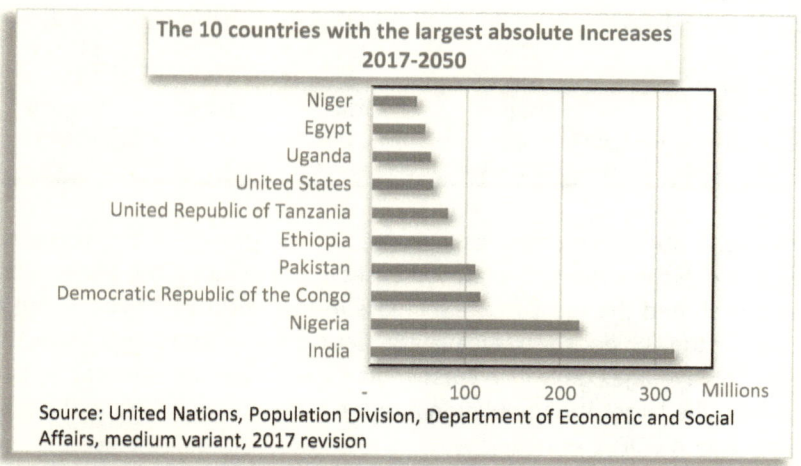

The 10 countries with the largest absolute Increases 2017-2050

Source: United Nations, Population Division, Department of Economic and Social Affairs, medium variant, 2017 revision

If we put the list of countries with the highest growth rates together with the list of countries with the highest contributions to the increase in the world's population, we obtain the list shown in Table 6.

What we observe in Table 6 is that, except for the US, all countries shown there are poor and generating large numbers of migrants – both of which are indicators of dissatisfaction with life back home. It is rather ironic then that the countries that can barely feed their people, and which are presently fraught with conflicts, are the ones expected to grow the most, both in relative and in absolute terms.

Why is migration a measure of dissatisfaction with life back home? Well, because most people will not willingly migrate to another country, where people speak a different language, worship a different God, and have a different culture, just to experience racial discrimination or be deprived of their rights as citizens. As such, we must conclude that at least for the millions who migrate, large families were not part of a conscious plan.

Table 6			
Country	GDP Per Capita (in PPP)	Migrant Stock Worldwide 2017	As a % of a country's total population 2017
Niger	$5,900	362,955	1.7%
Angola	$6,800	632,699	2.1%
Uganda	$2,400	739,667	1.7%
Somalia	$400	1,988,458	13.5%
D. R. Congo	$800	1,661,988	2.0%
Tanzania	$3,300	324,394	0.6%
Zambia	$4,000	275,089	1.6%
Mali	$2,200	1,066,120	5.7%
Burundi	$800	435,630	4.0%
Mozambique	$1,300	653,251	2.2%
Egypt	$13,000	3,412,957	3.5%
USA	$59,500	3,016,685	0.9%
Ethiopia	$2,100	800,879	0.8%
Pakistan	$5,400	5,978,635	3.0%
Nigeria	$5,900	1,255,425	0.7%
India	$7,200	16,587,720	1.2%

Source: UN, Population Division, Department of Economic and Social Affairs, medium variant; Trends in International Migrant Stock: 2017 revision; CIA, the World Factbook

How does one reconcile the migration statistics with the economic statistics of the USA? Americans migrate mainly to countries with lower GDP per capita (half of them go to Mexico, Canada, and Puerto Rico). As such, Americans migrate for non-economic reasons – some political, as would be the case of Americans in Canada, and some simply because they are ex-citizens of the countries to which they now return.

How do the countries in Table 6 fared in terms of internal and external conflicts? Here is a quick profile of each one of them:

Niger
- Tuareg rebellion of 2007-2009: The rebellion followed the government's failure to honor the 1995 agreement that gave the Tuareg people a bigger share of Niger's mineral resources[2].
- In 2016[3] the Diffa region received 105,000 Nigerian refugees who were fleeing the Boko Haram and another 121,000 internally displaced people. Boko Haram continues its attacks on refugees.

Angola[4]
- Ongoing guerilla warfare in the Cabinda province by a group that aims to gain independence.
- 1975-2002, the Angola Civil War

Uganda[5]
- Ongoing conflict between the Allied Democratic Forces and the governments of Uganda and D.R. Congo. The insurgency began in 1995 and intensified in 2013.
- Ongoing violence between the Konjo and Amba people in Uganda's capital. In 2016 thirty people died over election results.

Somalia[6]
- Ongoing civil war since 1991.
- An ongoing separatist insurgency in Ogaden that began in 1994.
- An ongoing war on terrorism that began in 2001.

D.R. Congo[7]
- 1998-2003 the second Congo war.
- Ongoing Allied Democratic Forces insurgency that began in 2007.
- A local dispute in Dongo over fishing rights that left 100 people dead and 168,000 displaced.
- A 2011 coup d'état attempt.
- Religious attacks in Kinshasa killing 101 people in 2013.

Tanzania[8]
- Although Tanzania has participated in several wars with neighboring countries, it has been spared the internal conflicts that blight other African countries.

---

[2] Wikipedia
[3] Peace Insight
[4] Wikipedia
[5] Wikipedia
[6] Wikipedia
[7] Wikipedia
[8] "Emerging Socio-Economic and Political Conflicts in Tanzania", William John, University for Peace & Conflict Monitor, *February 2011*.

- In 2008 the Prime Minister resigns and Cabinet gets dissolved due to extensive corruption. The 1995, 2000 and 2005 elections were all marred by violent conflicts with the opposition party.
- Conflicts between pastoralists and farmers in 2000 and again in 2008 due to water and land scarcity in the Kilosa District; 23 people die in both conflicts.
- 54 people die in a 1996 conflict between farmers and miners.
- Several conflicts between Barrick Gold and local communities. In 2008 a person dies and locals invade the mine to steal gold as pollution from the mine has destroyed their livelihood.

Mali[9]
- Ongoing Tuareg rebellion that began in 2012.
- An ongoing Islamist-nationalist conflict that began in 2012.

Burundi
- Civil war from 1993 to 2005.
- Following a disputed presidential election in 2005, violence erupts that carries into 2016; 600,000 people are displaced with 428,000 fleeing into Rwanda, Tanzania, Uganda, and D.R. Congo[10]. The number of deaths reaches 1,000.

Mozambique[11]
- 1977-1994, civil war.
- Ongoing guerrilla warfare by the Renamo rebels starting in 2013.
- Ongoing conflict, since 2007, between the government and an Islamist group that seeks to establish an Islamic state.

Egypt[12]
- A popular revolution in 2011 that overthrows the government.
- An ongoing conflict between Egyptian security forces and Islamic militants in the Sinai Peninsula starting in 2011.
- Popular uprising in 2011-2012 against President Morsi.
- Mass protests in 2013 against President Morsi again.
- Ongoing military interventions in Libya and Yemen.
- Ongoing political turmoil starting in 2013 with a military coup d'état.

Ethiopia[13]
- 1961-1991, Eritrean war of independence.
- 1974-1991, Ethiopian civil war.
- 1998-2000, Eritrean-Ethiopian war.
- An ongoing armed conflict since 1992 between the Oromo Liberation Front and the government.

---

[9] Wikipedia
[10] Global Conflict Tracker, November 2018
[11] Wikipedia
[12] Wikipedia
[13] Wikipedia

- An ongoing separatist movement in Ogaden that began in 1995.
- An ongoing US-lead operation (since 2002) to free the Horn of Africa from militant groups and pirates.

Pakistan[14]
- An ongoing cross-border conflict with India over Kashmir that has been going on for over 60 years.
- In 2009, fighting erupted between the group Tehrik-i-Taliban Pakistan and government forces that displaced three million people and caused extensive civilian deaths.
- Ongoing terrorism that since 2002, has killed 50,000 people.
- Ongoing sectarian and ethnic violence.

Nigeria[15]
- In North East Nigeria, 46% of households experienced at least one event of violence between 2010 and 2017; 73% of the conflicts are due to terrorism (Boko Haram).
- In North Central Nigeria, 25% of households experienced at least one event of violence between 2010 and 2017; 55% of the conflicts were due to disputes over land or access to resources and 21% were due to terrorism.
- An estimated 2,500 people died between 2010 and 2017 because of conflicts between herders and farmers.
- In South South Nigeria, 22% of households experienced violence; 32% of the conflicts were due to personal disputes and 36% were due to criminality.

India
- Ongoing ethnic and religious violence: Between 2005 and 2009, 650 people died and 11,000 were injured from communal riots.
- Ongoing conflicts over land acquisition and land-rivalry between "indigenous" and "migrant" communities. In 2017 there were 400 land disputes in India affecting six million people[16].

As Table 6 and the above country profiles show, large increases in the populations of poor countries have consequences not only for the country undergoing these changes but also for other countries. If country A is poor and experiences high population growth and country B is rich, or not rich but peaceful, it is only a matter of time before the residents of country A swarm the borders of country B – especially today when access to the Internet and to cheap transportation provide the residents of country A with a solution to their problem.

---

[14] Peace Insight, November 2018
[15] "Conflict and Violence in Nigeria", The World Bank and the National Bureau of Statistics Nigeria, 2018.
[16] Wikipedia

Table 7 shows the countries responsible for the most migrants in the world. This table shows the stock of migrants from a given country at a given year and not the annual flow, e.g., the first cell in the table indicates that in 1990 there were 6.7 million Indians living outside India.

In 2017, these nine countries accounted for 32% of the world's migrant stock and all of them, except for Russia, had an average GDP per capita much lower than the world's average ($23,350 for the world vs. $9,130 for the average of them; Russia = $27,900). Further, the populations of all of these countries, except those of Ukraine and Russia, grew between 1990 and 2017 at much higher rates than the world average.

Table 7: International Migrant Stocks Worldwide Millions							
Country of Origin	1990	2000	2010	2015	2017	% change 2017/90	% change in population 2017/90
India	6.7	8.0	13.3	15.9	16.6	147%	54%
Mexico	4.4	9.6	12.4	12.6	13.0	195%	51%
Russia	12.7	10.7	10.2	10.4	10.6	-16%	-2%
China	4.2	5.8	8.7	9.7	10.0	136%	20%
Bangladesh	5.5	5.4	6.7	7.3	7.5	38%	55%
Syria	0.6	0.7	1.1	6.2	6.9	1,006%	47%
Pakistan	3.3	3.4	5.0	5,9	6.0	79%	83%
Ukraine	5.6	5,6	5.5	5.8	5.9	7%	-14%
Philippines	2.0	3.1	4.7	5.4	5.7	180%	69%
World	152.5	172,6	220,0	247.6	257.7	69%	42%

Source: UN, Department of Economic and Social Affairs. Population Division (2017). Trends in International Migrant Stock: The 2017 revision

So, poverty and high population growth lead to more poverty which leads to local conflicts and to migration – not a very deep observation, but one that should be made.

Inequality

At this point, someone could argue that GDP per capita is not a very good indicator of an entire population's happiness because its distribution is not very equal. As such, a country could have a high GDP per capita, while at the same time a significant portion of its population could be living in poverty – the US is a good example of this (12.3% of its population lived in poverty in 2017 according to the US Census Bureau).

The Gini Index, on the other hand, measures the relative difference between the actual income distribution and the distribution where income (or wealth)

is equally distributed - in the sense that 10% of the population holds 10% of the income, 20% hold 20% of the income and so on. As such, a value of 100 means that a single person holds all of a country's income (i.e., the difference between the actual distribution and the equal distribution is at its maximum 100%), while a value of zero means that income is equally distributed (i.e., the difference between the actual distribution and the equal distribution is zero).

The World Bank provides estimates of the Gini Index but these estimates are distributed across countries and time periods in a way and make cross-country comparisons, or even comparisons of a country's progress through time, impossible. Nevertheless, the Gini Index could shed some light on Russia, Mexico, and Bangladesh.

In 1993, Russia's Gini Index was 48.4, while in 2015 in had declined to 37.7 – a 22% improvement! It is rather ironic that Russia under a "free market" system would achieve a more equal income distribution than it achieved under a communist regime! In any case, this could explain why Russia, with a relatively high GDP per capita, saw a massive exodus in 1990, when the Soviet Union fell, but then a 16% decline in its population living outside Russia in 2017 – things are getting better in Russia as far as the income distribution is concerned (and to think that people always view corruption as a bad thing!).

In 2000, when Mexico experienced a doubling of Mexicans living outside the country, the Gini Index for Mexico was 51.4 (even worse than Russia's), while in 2016 it was 43.4 – a 16% improvement which could explain, along with better enforcement of US immigration laws, why after 2010 the stock of Mexican migrants has remained stagnant.

Finally, Bangladesh's Gini Index went from 27.6 in 1991 to 32.4 in 2016 (a 17% deterioration). This could explain, along with its population growth and poverty, the 38% increase in migrants from Bangladesh between 1990 and 2017 (Note: a very low value for the Gini Index does not mean that every person is rich. As the Gini value for Bangladesh shows, income is relatively equally distributed, but this income is relatively low).

Although the countries in Table 7 generated the largest numbers of migrants, in most cases these migrants did not constitute a significant portion of those countries' populations. Table 8 shows the countries with the largest portion of their population living abroad. These countries, except for Kazakhstan and Romania, also have an average GDP per capita below the world average. Now, it is true that in some of these countries their citizens fled because of wars, or oppression. But wars and oppression are also, in large part, the result of grievances regarding resource allocations – that is certainly the case with

Palestinians and their dispute with Israel over land, as well as Jamaica, Bulgaria, Romania, Cuba and Mexico.

It is also true in countries where economic violence was disguised as ethnic hatred. For example, as J. Diamond writes in his book Collapse, "*the usual account of the genocides in Rwanda and Burundi portray them as the result of pre-existing ethnic hatreds fanned by cynical politicians for their own ends*". Politicians may have produced the spark, but as Diamond indicates the evidence point to the fact that the genocide in 1994 was the result of uncontrolled population growth, limited arable land, starvation, and a very unequal distribution of wealth.

Table 8		
Home Country	Worldwide migrants as a proportion of a country's home population, 2017	GDP per capita In 2017 PPP
State of Palestine	77%	$2,105
Jamaica	38%	$9,200
Syria	38%	$2,900
Kazakhstan	22%	$26,100
Bulgaria	18%	$21,600
Romania	18%	$24,000
Afghanistan	14%	$1,900
Cuba	14%	$12,300
Ukraine	13%	$8,700
Mexico	10%	$19,500

Source: UN, Department of Economic and Social Affairs. Population Division (2017). Trends in International Migrant Stock: The 2017 revision

In northwestern Rwanda where a study was conducted before and after the genocide (see Dimond) evidence show that Rwanda was a classical Malthusian case (see below for a discussion on Malthus): By 1983 food production per capita had dropped to the level of early 1960s, as population increased faster than food production, while the percent of young women living at home rose from 39% in 1988 to 67% in 1993 and that of young men from 73% to 100%.

This happened because young men found it difficult to acquire a farm, marry and leave home with all arable land already occupied. The average farm size decreased from 0.89 to 0.72 acre, and with more young people staying home, the average household size increased from 4.9 to 5.3 – meaning more people per family were now dependent on a smaller farm for their living. As a result, the percent of the population consuming calories less than the famine level increased from 9% in 1982 to 40% in 1990.

Finally, between 1988 and 1993, the percentage of large farms (bigger than 2.5 acres, which by Western standards is still way too small to support a family of 5.3 people – but then everything is relative) increased from 5% to 8% while the percentage of very small farms (smaller than 0.6 acres) increased from 36% to 45% contributing to inequality and resentment. An amazing 10% of households lived by stealing as they had neither farms nor any off-farm income.

When the genocide started in 1994, it was not only Hutus killing Tutsis and vice-a-versa. It also happened in the northwestern region that was exclusively occupied by Hutus. And in that region, it was Hutus killing Hutus, either to settle old scores or to decrease the number of dependents on the household farm.

Malthus

Some will consider the 9.8 billion people as an extinction level event, given that the current 7.6 billion of us have already managed to create substantial environmental problems. Yet others have a more optimistic view relying on science to solve any existing or future problem – including the creation of alternatives to the resources that are in limited supply. Anecdotal examples of past technological solutions are presented as "proof" that a technological fix is just around the corner for every conceivable problem.

These optimists neglect three points: First, that some problems do not have a technological fix, while those that do, cannot be implemented without additional resources being expended – resources that are diverted from other projects, or resources that sometimes generate other unforeseen problems (e.g., supplying surplus food to countries in Africa experiencing famine provided a short-term solution, but created a long-term problem by wiping out the local farmers and rendering these countries totally depended on food aid).

Second, the commercialization of these solutions takes a long time. And as we will see in the next sections, we only have less than 32 years before things begin to get extremely more unpleasant than they are now.

Finally, technological fixes are not always benign; invariably they are associated with detrimental side effects, e.g., nuclear waste as a by-product of clean nuclear power, organic, bacterial, and chemical pollution of ground and surface water as a by-product of increased agricultural output, and flooding of agricultural lands as a by-product of creating clean hydroelectric energy.

The debate on the optimal size of the population is an old one and goes back to Thomas Robert Malthus who in 1798 published a book entitled *An Essay on the Principle of Population*. In it, Malthus argued that although an increase in food production improves the people's general well-being, this increase is temporary as people start to have more children at a rate higher than that of food production and consequently, they bring their state of well-being back to the original level. So, according to Malthus, increases in well-being can be maintained only if the population does not increase, or if it increases at a rate lower than that of food production.

At one level, this is a rather simplistic view of the world. As economists have pointed out, Malthus' argument did not consider technological changes or capital investments, both of which transformed agriculture and resulted in a substantial increase in food production, especially after 1960 (the Green Revolution) – an increase that exceeded the growth in population.

In addition, at a country level, trade could ameliorate or eliminate food shortages. As noted earlier, the countries with the highest population growth were all located in the Arabian Peninsula where food production is very limited, but oil production is very high. Oil can then be traded for food and thus sustain the incredible growth rates in population that these countries experienced between 1950 and 2017. Actually, countries with a very high per capita income, and with an abundance of food production, such as the US, did not grow their populations as much as these Arab countries did. So, at the country level, population growth needs not be tied to food production. All one needs is some form of free trade.

It is also simplistic because someone's well-being does not depend solely on food consumption. If that was the case Mr. B. Gates and Mr. J. Bezos would have stopped trying to increase their net worth a very long time ago – how much could they possibly eat? Children have an intrinsic value (i.e., they are liked for their own sake), but also a social and economic value. At the time when Malthus wrote his book, having many children guaranteed that some of them would survive to adulthood and hence provide free labour to their parents' business as well as free care when their parents were old and frail.

Unfortunately, it appears that local habits have not caught up to the fact that the probability of survival of a child at birth has improved over the years because of better medicine. At the global level, mortality rates for infants over the last 27 years declined from 64.7 per 1,000 births in 1990 to 29.4 per 1,000 births in 2017 – that is a 55% reduction. Similar improvements are observed in all countries.

But at another level, there is a kernel of truth in what Malthus said. Sure, we can increase food production through technology, capital investment, and trade (trade is a solution only at the country level), but:

a) Eventually, food productivity at the world level will start to decline as we utilize less and less productive lands and exhaust the nutrients of the old lands.

   a.1. Although crop production per square kilometer of agricultural land has increased by 174% between 1961 and 2015 and meat production by 233%, there are worrisome signs on the horizon. First, there is climate change that will affect agricultural productivity by increasing the frequency of droughts and floods. An increase in the earth's temperature would also affect fish habitats and will also make crops more difficult to grow.

   a.2. Then there is soil erosion. According to Eurostat, 12.7% of the European Union's arable land – a land equal to the surface area of Greece – suffers from moderate to high erosion. The annual loss of soil in the EU due to water is 970 million tonnes. According to David Pimentel[17], the US is losing soil 10 times faster, India 40 times faster and China 30 times faster than the natural replenishment rate. Pimentel estimates that over the last 40 years, 30% of the world's arable land became unproductive due to soil erosion. According to the same author, it takes 500 years to replenish 1 inch of topsoil lost to erosion. As such, for all intents and purposes, soil is a non-renewable resource. In fact, between 1998 (when agricultural land achieved its maximum) and 2015, agricultural land globally declined by 1.6% while in the European Union it declined by 8.2%, in East Asia by 7.2%, in the Middle East and North Africa by 4% and in South Asia by 0.6%. It only increased in "Latin America & the Caribbean" by 6.2% – due to the mass deforestations in Brazil and other South American countries – and in Sub-Saharan Africa by 1.6%.

b) Food production has negative impacts on other aspects of the environment, impacts that accumulate over time.

   b.1. The world's forested area declined by 3% from 41.3 million km² in 1970 to 40 million km² in 2015 with consequences for air quality and soil erosion – that is 1.3 million square kilometers of forest, which is

---

[17] "Soil Erosion: A Food and Environmental Threat", the Journal of the Environment, Development and Sustainability (Vol. 8, 2006).

a bit bigger than the surface area of Peru. Much of this decline is due to clearing the land for agriculture and livestock ranching. Brazil alone lost 163,000 square miles of forest[18].

b.2. Agricultural methane emissions (a greenhouse gas that is 20-times more potent than CO_2 when it comes to climate change) increased by 18% from 2.9 billion metric tonnes of CO_2 equivalent gasses in 1970 to 3.4 billion metric tonnes in 2008; agricultural emissions of nitrous oxide (another greenhouse gas that kills the ozone in the atmosphere) increased by 67% from 1.3 billion metric tonnes in 1970 to 2.1 billion metric tonnes in 2008.

b.3. According to the Food and Agriculture Organization of the United Nations[19], "*Agriculture ... plays a major role in water pollution. Farms discharge large quantities of agrochemicals, organic matter, drug residues, sediments, and saline drainage into water bodies. The resultant water pollution poses demonstrated risks to aquatic ecosystems, human health and productive activities (UNEP, 2016). In most high-income countries and many emerging economies, agricultural pollution has already overtaken contamination from settlements and industries as the major factor in the degradation of inland and coastal waters (e.g. eutrophication). Nitrate from agriculture is the most common chemical contaminant in the world's groundwater aquifers (WWAP, 2013). In the European Union, 38 percent of water bodies are significantly under pressure from agricultural pollution (WWAP, 2015). In the United States of America, agriculture is the main source of pollution in rivers and streams, the second main source in wetlands and the third main source in lakes (US EPA, 2016). In China, agriculture is responsible for a large share of surface-water pollution and is responsible almost exclusively for groundwater pollution by nitrogen (FAO, 2013). ...Agricultural pressures on water quality come from cropping and livestock systems and aquaculture, which have all expanded and intensified to meet increasing food demand related to population growth and changes in dietary patterns....*"

c) Finally, our planet is a closed system (other than the sunlight and a few asteroids that fall on it) and as with all closed systems, there is a finiteness to it.

---

[18] World Bank, World Development Indicators
[19] Water Pollution from Agriculture, 2017, FAO

c.1. As mentioned above, the soil is, practically, a non-renewable resource and although there was some moderate increase in the amount of agricultural land from 1970 to 2000 (by 24%), it then declined by 2% between 2000 and 2015, at the time when the world's population increased by 20%. As a result, agricultural land per capita declined from 12.6 square meters in 1961 to 6.6 square meters in 2015 – a 48% decline.

c.2. Total freshwater withdrawals (by consumers, industry, and agriculture) increased by 36% between 1977 and 2014. This increased the proportion of renewable water resources being withdrawn from 5.5% in 1977 to 7.7% in 2014. Of that, 70% was withdrawn for food production (agriculture, livestock, and aquaculture). Given that the total fresh water is fixed, the freshwater resources available per capita have declined from 12,945 m^3 in 1977 to 7,500 m^3 in 2014.

So, every action has consequences in the form of water and air pollution, declines in the stocks of non-renewable resources, collapses of renewable resources due to over-extraction, extinction of other species, and the production of toxic chemicals that persist up the food chain. And all of these consequences will further limit the productivity of agriculture and aquaculture, as well as that of harvesting animals that live in the wild.

Are things likely to get better or worse as the population increases? This may sound like a trick question, on par with "will humans die if they stop breathing?", but given the paucity of unemotional discussion about population growth, it may be worth laying out the costs and benefits of population growth and consumption.

< Consumption >

"The best things in life aren't things."
— Art Buchwald, humorist, The Washington Post (1925-2007)

Summary

1. Our increased per capita prosperity between 1970 and 2016 contributed more to the overall increase in consumption than the growth in population.

2. Between 2016 and 2050 our increased per capita prosperity will contribute even more to the future overall increase in consumption than the growth in population.

3. Consumption in countries that were poor in 1970 – most of which were, in relative terms, still poor in 2016 – grew much faster than it did in rich countries.

4. In 2016, there was a very unequal distribution of expenditures around the world with the top 15 countries (5.1% of the world's population) accounting for 27.5% of the expenditures and the bottom 15 countries (4% of the world's population) accounting for 0.2% of them.

5. Inequality across countries, was worse than inequality within any single country of the world.

6. If near-equality is desirable at the world level, then, by 2050 expenditures will have to be four times larger than what they would have been based on historical patterns. In other words, if the money required to finance near-equality came from within the system, then the world economy would have to generate economic surpluses equal to four times its annual size on an annual basis – an economic impossibility.

The Past

When thinking of consumption, we need to identify two different impacts on its overall level: 1) the impact of more people and 2) the impact of increased consumption per person. This is so because if the goal was to reduce consumption, then reducing the number of people in the world will not be much of a benefit if those who remained increased their consumption enough to counter, or exceed, the decrease consumption due to the decrease in population.

Between 1970 and 2016 the world's consumption[20] (Gross National Expenditure, or GNE, measured in constant US$2010[21]) increased at an average annual rate of 3.0%, while population increased at 1.5%. So, consumption increased at double the population rate! As a result, average per capita consumption increased by 90% from $5,413 in 1970 to $10,296 in 2016 (in constant 2010 US$).

How much of the increase in expenditures ($57 trillion) is due to population growth and how much is due to the increase in the average per capita expenditures? If per capita expenditures had remained at the 1970 level, total expenditures in 2016 would have been $40 trillion instead of $77 trillion. As such, 64% of the increase is due to increased average spending per person and 36% is due to having more people on the planet. So, spending more per capita is a more significant contributor to increased overall consumption than population growth.

Table 9: Countries with the highest growth in real per capita GNE 1970-2016	
Lesotho	20,059%
Korea, Republic	918%
Indonesia	631%
Sri Lanka	617%
Malaysia	544%
India	444%
Thailand	390%
Singapore	364%
Dominican Republic	320%
Ireland	278%
Egypt	271%
Morocco	257%
Panama	261%
Rwanda	244%
Algeria	208%
Colombia	208%
Iceland	203%
Source: World Bank, World Development Indicators; UN Population Division, 2017 Revision	

---

[20] I will use the words "consumption" and "expenditures" interchangeably.
[21] GNE includes spending by consumers, government, and business on capital. It measures, more or less, the same thing that GDP does but from the expenditure side rather than the income side. Source: World Bank, World Development Indicators.

Per capita spending increased over the years not just in the rich countries of the West, but also in poor countries. As a matter of fact (see Table 9), the countries that grew the most in real (2010 US dollars) per capita expenditures were all poor countries, except for Iceland, Singapore, and Ireland. Other than Iceland and Ireland, there is no other Western country on this list. This is, of course, not surprising. Some of the countries in Table 9 were extremely poor back in 1970 and could only improve their status by increasing expenditures. Take for example Lesotho, a country in southern Africa. In 1970, Lesotho's GNE per capita was only $11 per year – 2,100 times lower than the GNE per capita of the United States. But, by 2016, Lesotho's GNE per capita was only 25 times smaller than the of the United States.

The Future

How are things likely to evolve over the 2017-2050 period when the population reaches 9.8 billion? We could use the past average growth rate of GNE and project it forward. But a look at the growth rates of GNE by decade, reveals that they steadily declined: starting at 3.8% during the 1970-1979 period and ending up with 2.74% during 2010-2016 period. As such, one would expect a further deterioration in the growth rate of GNE. Here we will take the average annual rate for the period 2017-2050 to be 2.6%, which is lower than other forecasts (Citibank predicts 4.2%, IMF 3.7% (to 2023) and OECD 3.0%) – in other words, we will play it conservatively.

In this scenario then (we will call it **Scenario 1**), consumption, in constant 2010 US dollars, will reach $186 trillion by 2050 – a number that is 828% bigger than the level of consumption in 1970 and 142% bigger than that of 2016. In this scenario, 78% of the total increase in consumption will be due to the increase in the average per capita spending and 22% will be due to the growth in population.

That is great, one might exclaim! Even with inequality being a cruel spoiler, this huge increase in expenditures is bound to reach every person on the planet, right? Well, yes, but we do not know the extent of the reach since data on income distribution, as mentioned earlier, are in a state of disarray. Not every country reports the data needed to construct the Gini Index and those who do, are reporting them intermittently (they are also problems with bad methodologies or with cheating as was the case of Greece that made up its economic data in order to enter the EU Zone). As such, neither for many single countries nor for many regional aggregates can we tell in a systematic way how much better, or worse, things are getting over time.

With this cautionary note in mind, of the 142 countries that have more than one year of data, 53, or 37%, saw their Gini Index deteriorate over time (at least over the few years in the World Bank database). The most recent values for the Gini Index range from a low 25.4% for Slovenia, which is good, to a high of 57.1% for Zambia, which is bad.

How would an income distribution with a Gini Index equal to 57.1% look like? Consider a country with five individuals with the following incomes (not necessarily the only distribution with a Gini Index equal to 57.1%):

Individuals	Income	Proportion of total income received by an individual
Individual 1	$15	5.7%
Individual 2	$15	5.7%
Individual 3	$15	5.7%
Individual 4	$15	5.7%
Individual 5	$202	77.1%

In the above example, 20% of the people (one person in our case) received 77.1% of the aggregate income, while 80% received 22.9% of it. The Gini Index of this distribution has a value of 57.1%, and what it says is that this income distribution differs from an equal distribution by 57.1%.

One could use the Gini Index not only to measure economic disparity within a country but also across countries. Table 10 shows the per capita consumption, in constant US dollars, for the top fifteen and the bottom fifteen countries in the world. Monaco, the top country, consumes 2,130 times more per capita than the bottom country, Somalia.

The top 15 countries, which account for 5.1% of the world's population (84% of their population is just the population of the US), account for 27.5% of the world's total consumption. On the other hand, the bottom 15 countries, which account for a similar proportion of the world's population (4%), account for just 0.2% of the world's consumption! In other words, the top 15 countries consume 139 times more per capita than the bottom 15 countries.

So, the distribution of per capita expenditures around the world is nowhere near equality. As a matter of fact, its Gini Index is 74.4%, a value much worse than any single country in the world.

To achieve equality at the world level we will have to distribute GNE equally not only among the populations of each country but also across the populations of different countries. If we were able to distribute GNE across countries so that they all have the same per capita consumption, then it is feasible for these countries to redistribute it equally among their citizens so that everyone across the world enjoys the same amount of consumption – at least in theory.

Country	2016 GNE per capita in 2010 $	Proportion of population accounted for by:	Proportion of GNE accounted for by:
Table 10: Top and bottom 15 countries			
Top 15		5.1%	27.5%
Monaco	151,251		
Liechtenstein	104,763		
Isle of Man*	84,046		
Norway	83,714		
Luxembourg	72,470		
Switzerland	66,612		
Channel Islands*	62,421		
Gibraltar*	61,700		
Bermuda	59,719		
Denmark	57,010		
Ireland	56,520		
Greenland	56,073		
Australia	55,044		
USA	54,527		
Sweden	54,157		
Bottom 15		4.0%	0.2%
Uganda	721		
Afghanistan	691		
Guinea-Bissau	677		
Gambia	630		
Liberia	602		
Malawi	601		
Sierra Leone	598		
Eritrea	489		
Yemen	481		
Niger	462		
Madagascar	448		
D.R. Congo	448		
C.A.R.	410		
Burundi	258		
Somalia	71		

Source: World Bank, Development Indicators; United Nations, UNData
*For the Isle of Man, the Channel Islands, and Gibraltar, I used GDP per capita

But, what level of per capita consumption would satisfy our notion of equality across countries? Well, there is no answer to that, at least not a "scientific" answer. We could re-distribute income to the point where the increase in consumption from the extra income given to the poor countries is equal to the reduced consumption from the loss of income in rich countries. But this is an efficiency argument and not an equity argument.

As such, it will have to be arbitrary. But what? Well, before we get to this, a point of clarification: whatever we do, it cannot involve going into a rich country, grabbing its money, and giving it to a poor country. Why? Because a) there is no mechanism for doing so, and b) this procedure is unlikely to receive majority approval as people are concerned with fair procedures – and this is far from a fair procedure.

If we increased everyone's per capita spending to match that of the top country in the world (Monaco), then the resources required will be too high. In addition, it could create a sense of unfairness as we will be subsidizing some very rich countries (like Liechtenstein, Isle of Man, and Norway, see Table 10) that need no subsidy. If, on the other hand, we only increased the per capita spending of those below the world average to match that average, then the resulting Gini Index will be too high as nearly half of the world's countries have a per capita GNE higher than the world average. So, it must be an average that is close to that enjoyed by a rich country but not too high. Here we will use the United States as our arbitrary reference country. And since it presently ranks as 14th in the world with respect to consumption per capita, it is a conservative reference country.

Before deciding on the actual dollar value that each country will receive, we will have to find out what will happen by 2050 in the absence of interference. As we mentioned above, if the world grows at an average of 2.6% per annum, then by 2050 GNE will be equal to $186 trillion. But some countries will grow faster than 2.6% per annum and some will grow slower. And these differential growth rates are bound to change the distribution of GNE per capita for all countries. As such, poor countries may require fewer transfer payments at the endpoint – as was the case with Lesotho between 1970 and 2016.

Among the various country-groupings that the World Bank puts together, there is one where countries are grouped by income. Table 11 shows the growth rates from 1970 to 2016 of these income groups. What we observe in Table 11 is that in high-income countries consumption increased at a much slower rate than it did in all the other income groups. This makes intuitive sense: rich countries have already fully utilized their natural and human resources and that is why they are rich. But at the same time, this provides them with fewer opportunities for high growth.

This is also true across time. That is, in the past, when the rich countries were not as rich, they grew faster than they do today. For example, from 1970 to1980, consumption for the high-income group grew at 3.3% per annum; from 1980 to 1990 it grew at 3.1% per annum, from 1990 to 2000 it grew by 2.7% per annum, and from 2000 to 2010 at 1.6% per annum (between 2010 and 2016 it grew by 1.7% per annum but the decade is not over yet). In other words, in every successive decade, the growth rate of this group's consumption decreased by 0.43 percentage points.

	Table 11	
Income Group	Average annual rate of change in GNE 1970-2016	Average annual rate of change in GNE 2017- 2050
High income	2.5%	1.7%
Upper middle income	6.2%	4.1%
Middle income	5.5%	3.7%
Lower middle income	5.0%	3.4%
Low income	5.0%	3.4%
Source: The World Bank; the projections are mine		

In estimating what each income group's consumption will be in 2050, I used 1.7% per annum as the average annual growth rate for the high-income group and then adjusted the other income groups' rates according to the relationship their rates had to the high-income group's during the 1970-2016 period. The result appears in the second column of Table 11.

If we grow the 2016 consumption expenditures of each country within these income groups by the rates shown in Table 11, then in 2050 we get again the $186 trillion – the same amount we got earlier by using just one average growth figure (2.6%) for the world's total consumption.

Following this procedure, then, by 2050 the US' per capita consumption will reach $79,961 and the country will rank 16th in the world, as opposed to 14th in 2016. This is because the US population will grow faster than the populations of the other high-income countries.

What will happen to the world's total consumption if we leave the 15 countries above the US alone (and thus avoid using unfair procedures), but intervene annually with all the other countries in order to increase their per capita consumption to $79,961? To simplify things, we will use "divine" money for the intervention, i.e., money coming from outside the system. Our goal here is not to find a mechanism for achieving equality, but rather to find out whether near-equality is economically feasible and whether there are environmental consequences due to the increased consumption.

Well, the answer is that by 2050 total world consumption will reach $784 trillion – that is a 920% higher than it was in 2016. And the Gini Index will be

0.3% – nearly zero, nut not zero because of the 15 countries with higher per capita consumption than the US. We will call this **Scenario 2**. Under this scenario, when 2050 arrives, 1.8% of the population (this is the population of the top 15 rich countries) will spend 2.1% of the world's GNE, while 98.2% of the population will spend 97.9% of its GNE – a near equality for all!

The difference between the $784 trillion (what GNE will need to be in order to achieve near equality) and the $186 trillion (what GNE is going to be without any attempts to intervene) is the price of equality. This price is $598 trillion.

How much is $598 trillion? Well, it is 7.8 times bigger than the world's entire GNE in 2016! In other words, the world will need to produce for almost 8 years and not consume anything, including food, in order to finance just a year of it. Since this is not an economic model that makes any sense (except perhaps in Stalin's Soviet Union), equality from an economic perspective is not feasible.

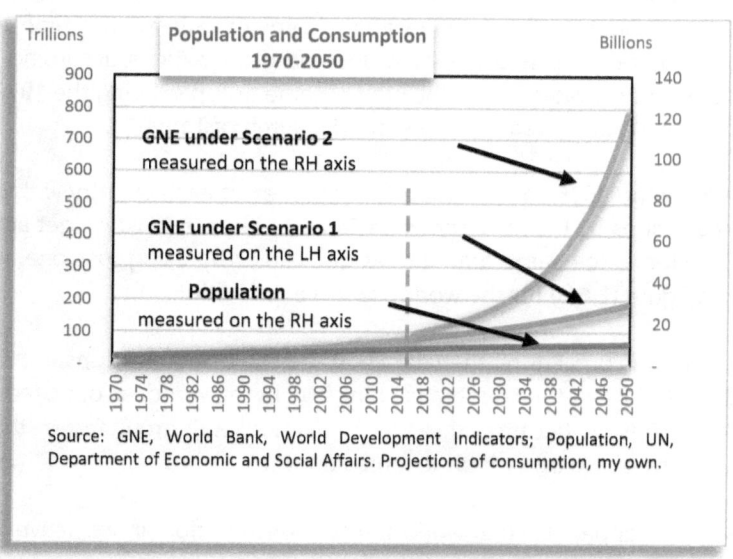

Source: GNE, World Bank, World Development Indicators; Population, UN, Department of Economic and Social Affairs. Projections of consumption, my own.

< Impacts >

"A very Faustian choice is upon us: whether to accept our corrosive and risky behavior as the unavoidable price of population and economic growth or to take stock of ourselves and search for a new environmental ethic."
— E. O. Wilson, biologist (1929 -)

Summary

1. If the economy continues to grow as expected, by 2050 the world would need to spend annually almost the entire GDP of the United States to compensate for the annual costs of climate change and other pollutants.

2. If in addition we adjust for near-equality, then the world will need to spend annually twice the 2017 world GDP to compensate for the costs of climate change and other pollutants. In other words, the entire world will have to work thrice per year just to pay the annual costs of its annual consumption! A rather Kafkaesque affair.

3. If things continue at the present speed, the annual deaths due to pollution and climate change will reach 25.7 million people. If we also adjust for near equality, the annual deaths will reach 69.8 million people (a number that is 16% higher than the total number of people who died during the six years of WWII).

4. If things continue at the present speed, 99% of the mammal species that were around in 2016 will be extinct by 2050 and so will 47% of all the fish species, 6.3% of all the plant species and 39.3% of all the bird species. If equality is also desired then all the mammal species, all the fish species, all the bird species and 50% of the plant species will be extinct by 2050 due to climate change and other human activities.

5. If things continue at the present pace, 83% of the world's population in 2050 will be experiencing health problems (lung and heart diseases, malnutrition, diarrhea, asthma, and cholera, dengue, and malaria infections) because of climate change and general pollution, while under near-equality everyone will be experiencing health problems.

6. If things continue as they are, there will be mass migrations and local conflicts involving at least 3.8 billion people, while an attempt at equality will increase this number to 9.7 billion (out of 9.8 billion) – if only Dante was around to see it!

7. Environmental impacts affect the poor countries of the world, such as those in Africa and Asia, more than the rich countries. This implies that attempting equality will not only fail but will also hurt more those in need of help.

8. Equality aside, things cannot possibly continue at the present speed. None of the economic or demographic forecasts presented in this book will materialize given the economic costs, the deteriorating health of large sections of the population, the number of deaths and the elimination of most of the other species. Eventually, population and economic growth will stall and begin to decline whether we like it or not. If all roads lead to Rome then, why not stay on the path where GDP and population are lower, and avoid the path that leads to the same result but only after a lot of pain?

Now if you were an optimist, who believed in the power of science, or maybe in God's invisible hand, then you would take Scenario 2 as good news and exclaim, "That's all great! Everyone will live like a king!". But we have already seen that Scenario 2 is not feasible from an economic perspective. Are Scenarios 1 and 2 feasible from an impact perspective?

Greenhouse Gas Emissions – aka Climate Change

The amount of greenhouse gas emissions per dollar of expenditure has been declining over the years at an average annual rate of 1.3% – due perhaps to better technologies or perhaps due to policy measures: it was 1.38 kilograms of CO_2 equivalent gas per dollar of GNE in 1970 and 0.77 kilograms in 2012 – a 43% decline.

The graph below shows the historical amounts of greenhouse gasses and my projections[22] to 2050 based on our two scenarios of future GNE. By 2050, we

---

[22] My forecast is based on the following equation:
(Greenhouse gasses) = 17,672,231,461 + 0.000511123*(GNE). This equation has an R^2 = 97.2%, i.e., it explains 97.2% of the variation in the data and it says that for every $1 million dollar increase in GNE, greenhouse gasses increase by 511 kilograms.

will be producing 0.6 kilograms of greenhouse gas emissions per dollar of GNE - a decline of 22% over 2012, which is in the ballpark with the previous reduction over a similar time period (36% from 1974 to 2012).

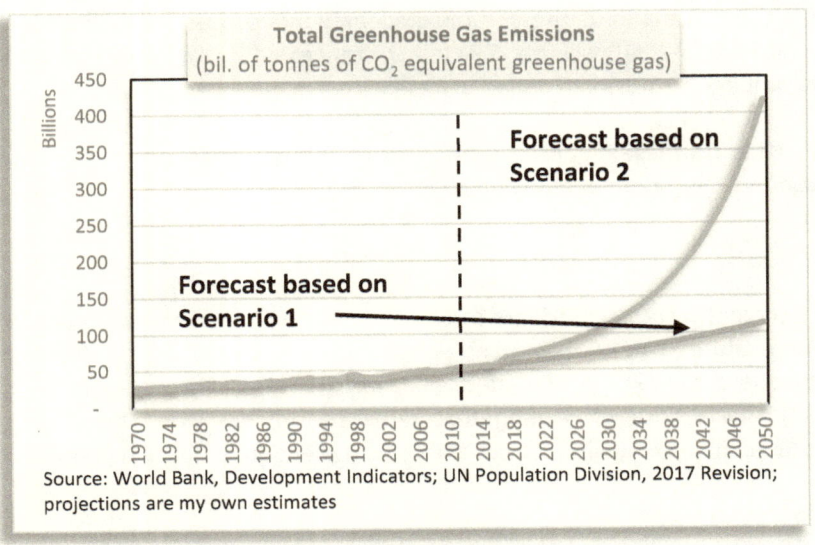

Source: World Bank, Development Indicators; UN Population Division, 2017 Revision; projections are my own estimates

So, under Scenario 1 (where consumption increases on average by 2.6% per year) greenhouse gas emissions in 2050 will be 307% higher per annum than they were in 1970 and 110% higher than they were in 2012 – reaching 113 billion tonnes of CO_2 equivalent greenhouse gasses.

Under Scenario 2 (where consumption increases by 2.6% per annum and we make an annual adjustment for equality), annual greenhouse gas emissions in 2050 will be 1,412% higher than they were in 1970 and 681% higher than they were in 2012 – reaching 418 billion tonnes of CO_2 equivalent greenhouse gasses!

For greenhouse gas emissions it is important to add up the annual emissions as these gasses stay in the atmosphere for a long time. For example, 65-80% of the CO_2 gas gets absorbed by water (which is good on the one hand but bad on the other because it increases the acidification of the oceans), but only after 20-200 years. The remaining 20-35% gets absorbed over thousands of years. Methane lasts for about 12 years, while nitrous oxide is destroyed through chemical reactions in about 114 years. So, except for methane, which accounted only for 5.8% of greenhouse gasses in 2008, all the other greenhouse gasses persist over the period of analysis used here.

Based on Scenario 1, the accumulated total greenhouse gas emissions for the 2013-2050 period will be 3 trillion tonnes - 81% more than the accumulated emissions for the 1970-2012 period.

Based on Scenario 2, the accumulated greenhouse gas emissions for the period 2013-2050 will be 5.9 trillion tonnes - 259% higher than the accumulated emissions for the 1970-2012 period.

So, what do these higher levels of greenhouse gas emissions imply for the world's average temperature?

୧୭ஜ☙②

According to NASA's Goddard Institute for Space Studies, the average global temperature (over both land and ocean) increased by 0.3°C in 1970 over the average of the 1951-1980 period, while in 2012 it increased by 0.62°C — i.e., its increase doubled. During that same period, the world produced an accumulated 1.65 trillion tonnes of CO_2 equivalent greenhouse gas emissions.

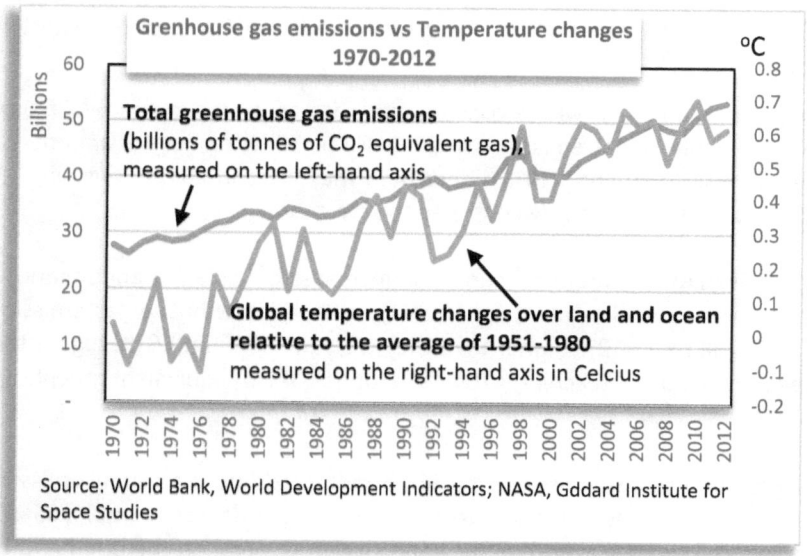

Source: World Bank, World Development Indicators; NASA, Gddard Institute for Space Studies

The graph above shows the relationship between greenhouse gas emissions and temperature changes over the reference period. It is clear in the graph that both variables trend upwards – actually, the temperature increases faster than the greenhouse gas emissions, perhaps due to the cumulative impact that greenhouse gasses have.

But one might argue that a lot of things in life trend upward without necessarily having a causal relationship. For example, the number of Internet users since 2000 also trends upward, but it does not mean that Internet users cause the global temperature to go up. In this case, however, there seems to be a near-unanimous agreement among scientists[23] that greenhouse gasses cause the temperature to go up because they generate a kind of greenhouse effect, trapping the heat from sun – hence the name: *"Radiative forcing (RF) quantifies the change in energy fluxes caused by changes in these drivers... Positive RF leads to surface warming, negative RF leads to surface cooling... Total radiative forcing is positive and has led to an uptake of energy by the climate system. The largest contribution to total radiative forcing is caused by the increase in the atmospheric concentration of CO_2 since 1750"* (Intergovernmental Panel on Climate Change, 2013).

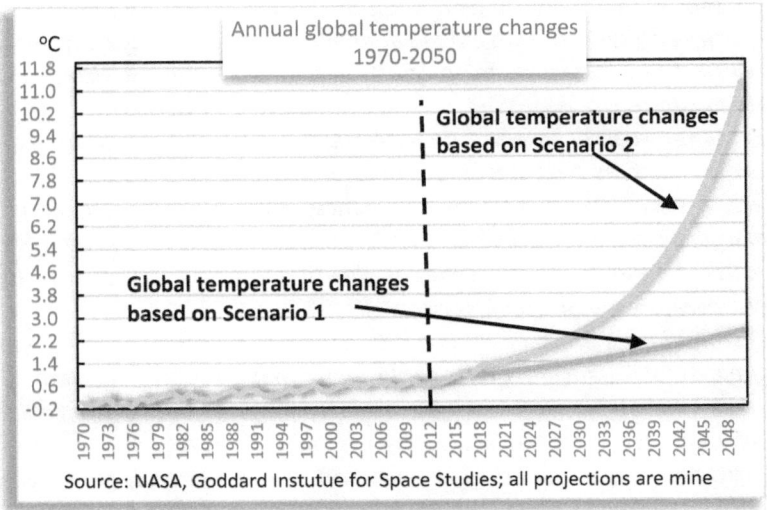

The graph above shows the historical temperature changes over the average of the years 1951-1980 and my projections based on our two scenarios[24].

---

[23] NASA, Global Climate Change, Scientific Consensus: Earth's Climate is Warming: *"Multiple studies published in peer-reviewed scientific journals show that 97 percent or more of actively publishing climate scientists agree: Climate-warming trends over the past century are extremely likely due to human activities. In addition, most of the leading scientific organizations worldwide have issued public statements endorsing this position"*

[24] My projections were derived using the following equation:
(Change in temperature) = -0.764104 + 0.00000000002861*(Greenhouse gasses). This equation has an R^2 of 87.2%. The R^2 shows how much of the variation in the data is explained by the equation – in this case, 87.2%. The equation says that for every 1 billion tonnes of greenhouse gasses, the temperature increases by 0.029 degrees Celsius.

According to Scenario 1, the global temperature by 2050 will increase by 2.46°C over the reference period. That is 176% higher than it was in 2017.

Under Scenario 2, it would increase by 11.2°C or 1,159% more than its 2017 level!

What is the impact of an increase in temperature by 1° Celsius? In the "Summary for Policymakers" of the IPCC report, we get a qualitative assessment but no hard numbers. These are the five IPCC statements of concern:

1) *Unique and threatened systems: Some unique and threatened systems, including ecosystems and cultures, are already at risk from climate change (high confidence). The number of such systems at risk of severe consequences is higher with additional warming of around 1°C. Many species and systems with limited adaptive capacity are subject to very high risks with additional warming of 2°C, particularly Arctic-sea-ice and coral-reef systems.*
2) *Extreme weather events: Climate-change-related risks from extreme events, such as heat waves, extreme precipitation, and coastal flooding, are already moderate (high confidence) and high with 1°C additional warming (medium confidence). Risks associated with some types of extreme events (e.g., extreme heat) increase further at higher temperatures (high confidence).*
3) *Distribution of impacts: Risks are unevenly distributed and are generally greater for disadvantaged people and communities in countries at all levels of development. Risks are already moderate because of regionally differentiated climate-change impacts on crop production in particular (medium to high confidence). Based on projected decreases in regional crop yields and water availability, risks of unevenly distributed impacts are high for additional warming above 2°C (medium confidence).*
4) *Global aggregate impacts: Risks of global aggregate impacts are moderate for additional warming between 1–2°C, reflecting impacts to both Earth's biodiversity and the overall global economy (medium confidence). Extensive biodiversity loss with associated loss of ecosystem goods and services results in high risks around 3°C additional warming (high confidence). Aggregate economic damages accelerate with increasing temperature (limited evidence, high agreement), but few quantitative estimates have been completed for additional warming around 3°C or above.*
5) *Large-scale singular events: With increasing warming, some physical systems or ecosystems may be at risk of abrupt and irreversible changes. Risks associated with such tipping points become moderate between 0–1°C additional warming, due to early warning signs that both warm-water*

coral reef and Arctic ecosystems are already experiencing irreversible regime shifts (medium confidence). Risks increase disproportionately as temperature increases between 1–2°C additional warming and become high above 3°C, due to the potential for a large and irreversible sea level rise from ice sheet loss. For sustained warming greater than some threshold, near-complete loss of the Greenland ice sheet would occur over a millennium or more, contributing up to 7 m of global mean sea level rise.

Although written in a mind-twisting style and language, the IPCC report says that basically things are not very good right now and they will get worse if the temperature rises by another 1-2°C. Further, they will become catastrophic if the temperature rises by 3°C or more.

So, let us see if we could put some numbers around the above statements:

1) **Loss of biodiversity and food sources**:

According to the first statement of concern, an increase in temperatures by 1°C is associated with a high probability for severe consequences for some ecosystems and an increase of 2°C is associated with a very high probability for severe consequences. According to the World Bank, in 2017 the following number of species were considered threatened:

a. 3,434 mammal species, or 63% of all mammal species on earth[25]: the number of mammal species threatened in middle and low-middle income countries combined, was 45% greater than those threatened in low, low-middle, lower-middle, upper-middle, and high-income countries combined. These observations seem to imply that "no development" means no threats to mammals, while "beginning to develop" means increased threats to mammal species, and finally, "full development" means no threats to mammal species because there is no one left to threaten!

    And just in case you thought that the list of threatened species contains just weird frogs, the Red List of Threatened Species, published by the International Union for Conservation of Nature (IUCN), lists, among other mammals, 31 deer species, 6 bison species, 11 species of rabbits, 4 species of elk, 39 species of dolphin and 58 species of whales, the African elephant and the Asian elephant – species that are used by humans for food, clothing, fire and other purposes;

---

[25] Mammal Species of the World, 3rd Edition, Wilson and Reeder, 2005

b. 8,232 fish species, or 30% of all fish species[26]. Using the IUCN Red List again, we find, among other things, 18 species of sea bass, 85 species of trout, 383 species of crab, 152 species of flounder, 2 species of halibut, 60 species of sole and 95 species of shrimp and prawns;

c. 15,735 plant species, or 4% of all plant species[27]. Again, using the IUCN Red list of threatened species, we find, among others, 6 species of wheat, 28 species of rice and 49 species of peas; and

d. 4,584 bird species, or 25% of all bird species[28], including the mallard duck, two species of wild turkey, 79 species of quails, 36 species of goose, 8 species of guinea fowl and 8 species of partridges.

Now, not all the threatened species are threatened solely by climate change and its derivatives (droughts, forest fires, warm water, etc.). They are also threatened by other human activities, such as logging and development, that destroy their habitat, and by overfishing and poaching that destroy the species directly. But since we are trying to evaluate the impacts of more people and more consumption (and hence more development) on other species, we will combine the impacts due to temperature increase with those of other human activities.

So, under Scenario 1, the temperature increases by 2.46°C in 2050, or 1.57°C above the 2017 level – the year when all these species were threatened. This increase then is 57% higher than the 1°C, which was associated with high probability of severe consequences for biodiversity. Hence, 1.57°C above the 1°C threshold is associated with a probability that is between high and very high for severe consequences – which we take it here to mean the extinction of species that were already threatened in 2017.

If the relationship between threatened species, extinct species, and temperature is linear, then from the number of species we had in 2017 we would expect to lose:
- 99% of the mammal species and render the remaining 1% threatened,
- 47% of the fish species and render remaining 53% threatened,
- 6.3% of the plant species and render another 11% threatened and
- 39.3% of the bird species and render the remaining 60.7% threatened.

Under Scenario 2, which is 10.31°C above the 2017 level, we would expect to lose:

---

[26] Florida Museum, website

[27] Royal Botanical Gardens, Kew

[28] American Museum of Natural History

- all the mammal species (except us naturally),
- all the fish species,
- 50% of all plant species and render the remaining 50% threatened, and
- all the bird species.

Finally! For the first time in human history, we will have the planet to ourselves – with a few weeds and other noxious plants to keep us company! Who knows, maybe the cockroaches and other obnoxious insects will survive as a punishment for our hubris!

◦⑨�୧୨②

According to the Food and Agriculture Organization of the United Nations (FAO), 822 million people in the world were undernourished in 2016. This was up from 783.7 million people in 2014. This is rather ironic given that, as we will see in the Food Section below, per capita food production increased substantially. Table 12 shows the distribution of undernourished (aka hungry) people by region.

Table 12: Undernourished People by Region 2016		
Region	Proportion	Number
World	11.0%	821,882,654
Northern Africa	8.5%	19,497,776
Eastern Africa	31.6%	129,761,604
Middle Africa	25.7%	40,750,685
Southern Africa	8.2%	5,271,974
Western Africa	12.8%	46,361,802
Central Asia	6.0%	4,187,266
Southern Asia	15.1%	278,786,262
Western Asia	11.1%	29,186,119
East Asia & Southeast Asia	8.9%	203,247,905
Caribbean	17.1%	7,455,914
Central America	6.3%	11,024,292
South America	4.9%	20,602,444
Oceania	6.6%	2,647,751
North America & Europe	< 2.5%	23,100,860
Source: FAO for proportions of undernourished people; UN for population estimates, 2017 Revision		

The reduction in species through droughts, wildfires, floods, hurricanes, winter storms and increased water temperature and other human activities will result in a reduction in the available food supply – especially in regions where people don't buy their food at the store, but rather grow it, or hunt and fish for it – and as such, we expect the proportion of undernourished people to increase more in poor countries.

Several studies have shown that food from animal sources is associated with better growth, cognitive function, activity, pregnancy outcomes, and morbidity. In a Kenyan study[29], the children who ate meat gained 30% to 80% more weight than the control group, while those who drank milk gained 40% more than the other group.

As such, when fish and meat production declines – and as we saw, climate change will affect fish and meat more severely than crops – we expect the proportion of undernourished people to increase by more than the overall reduction in food. We have included in our calculations an additional 30% impact under Scenario 1 (the lower limit of the Kenyan study) and a 55% impact under Scenario 2 (when there will be no meat or fish available and hence no eggs or milk either) to capture this effect. Assuming that the number of species is proportional to the food production, food production will decline by 11% under Scenario 1 and by 56% under Scenario 2.

As such, under Scenario 1 the number of undernourished people will increase to 18% of the population, reaching 1.7 billion people in 2050 (879 million additional over 2016). Of those, 1.095% will die (The Borgen Project), or 19.3 million people (10 million additional over 2016).

In terms of the economic costs of Scenario 1, since undernourished people are not very productive, the economy will lose their contributions. Using the regional GDP per capita, we get a total opportunity cost of US$7.7 trillion in 2050 (in 2010 US dollars) – US$4 trillion additional costs over 2016, without counting any medical care costs or the value of human life.

Under Scenario 2, the number of undernourished people would reach 2.9 billion (2.1 billion additional), or 30% of the world population in 2050, with 32.2 million deaths (23 million additional deaths). In terms of the economic costs of Scenario 2, they will reach US$12.9 trillion (in 2010 US dollars) – US$9.3 trillion additional – without counting medical costs or the value of human life.

Now, these estimates could severely underestimate what would happen under the two scenarios. The reason being that we have not examined which species will become extinct and which ones will survive. This analysis would take too much effort to compute and is beyond the scope of this book. But if the plants, fishes, and birds that survive under Scenario 1, and the plants under Scenario 2, are not edible, or are species that cannot be cultivated *en*

---

[29] Grillenberger M, Neumann CG, Murphy SP, Bwibo NO, van't Veer P, et al. (2003) Food supplements have a positive impact on weight gain and the addition of animal source foods increases lean body mass of Kenyan schoolchildren. J. Nutr. 133: 3957S-3964S.

masse (e.g., we cannot breed whales in ponds), then that basically signals the end of the human species as well.

2) Extreme weather

According to the second statement of concern, extreme weather events are already moderate but as temperature increases by an additional 1°C they will become very frequent, and then extremely frequent when the temperatures increase more than 1°C.

a. **Heatwaves:** The number of heatwaves in the US, i.e., when the temperature is far above the average for a time period, has been increasing over the years, and the number of extreme heatwaves (more than 100° F days) has tripled compared to the long-term average. The land area that experiences much above average temperatures during summers increased from 4.5% during the 1960s to 23% during the 2010-2017 period.

   In 2017, 2,993 people died in the US due to heatwaves[30] and according to the World Health Organization (WHO), 70,000 people died in Europe during the 2003 heatwave. Over 125 million of vulnerable adults around the world were exposed to heatwaves between 2000 and 2016[31].

   At the world level, between 1995 and 2015, 148,000 people died from heatwaves according to the Centre for Research on the Epidemiology of Disasters (CRED)[32]. This same report also indicates that high-income countries account for most of these deaths with Europe alone accounting for 90%. Of course, this could simply "appear" to be so because there are no data reported for Africa, West Asia, and Central and South America.

   Annual data by country on heat-related deaths are not available (except for the US). For some countries, researchers estimate these deaths by looking at the number of people who died due to coronary and respiratory causes during a heatwave and then deduce, if these deaths were higher than the periods without heatwaves, that the extra deaths were "caused" by the heatwave. However, this procedure, apart from being an inference rather than real numbers, does not tell us how many people died in a heatwave. Instead, it tells us how many additional

---

[30] Billion-Dollar Disasters report, NIDIS, 2017
[31] Information and public health advice: heat and health
[32] "The Human Costs of Weather-Related Disasters", CRED.

people with coronary and/or respiratory problems died during a heatwave over the average of the period without a heatwave.

A rather painful search of academic and news articles, as well as data from the CDC, WHO and the Indian government indicate that the total number of deaths for the period 1995-2015 was 313,000 - more than double the CRED estimate provided above.

The average increase in temperature for the period 1995-2015 was 0.58°C, while under Scenario 1 the average of the 2030-2050 decade will be 1.86°C – that is 3.2 times higher than the 1995-2015 average. If the relationship between heat-related deaths and temperature is proportional (we cannot derive quantitative estimates for this relationship because we only have one total number of deaths for the period), then during the 2030-2050 period total deaths would rise to 1,005,429, or 50,721 per year.

Under Scenario 2, the average temperature increase during the 2030-2050 period will be 5.54°C or 9.6 times greater than the average of the 1995-2015 period. As such, deaths due to heatwaves under this scenario would increase to 2,987,495, or 149,375 per year.

The above estimates are probably conservative because while the temperature is increasing, the proportion of the world's population that lives in urban centers is also increasing – from 44.7% in 1995 to 54.7% in 2017 and to 65.3% in 2050 (my estimate). Urbanization makes the effects of heatwaves worse because: a) cities retain more of the heat and b) urban air pollution creates smog which accentuates respiratory and heart problems.

◦◦⑨⁂ஐ②

In addition to killing people, extreme heat is also associated with economic losses:

a) There are significantly more people than those who die who go to a hospital for treatment. According to a US study[33], for every person that dies, 54 go to a hospital for treatment – 73,180 Americans were hospitalized during 2001-2010. Using this ratio at the global level, we estimate that in 2050, 2,739,000 people will be hospitalized for

---

[33] Economic Burden of Hospitalizations for Heat-Related Illnesses in the United States, 2001–2010, Michael T. Schmeltz, Elisaveta P. Petkova, and Janet L. Gamble, Int J Environ Res Public Health. 2016 Sep; 13(9): 894.

heat-related illness under Scenario 1, and 8,066,000 people under Scenario 2.

The same US study also indicates that the average cost for treating people with heat-related illnesses was $5,359 per person. But since countries with lower per capita GDP than the US are expected to have lower hospitalization costs, we used here the average global costs of $1,094 per person. This number is obtained by multiplying the US costs per patient by 20% (which is the ratio of global GDP per capita to the US GDP per capita).

This procedure then produces estimates for the annual hospitalization costs in 2050 of $3.0 billion under Scenario 1 and $8.8 billion under Scenario 2.

b) During heat waves, people increase their use of air-conditioners. A utility company in the US reported that on average its clients in four US cities in the south paid $29 more in June of 2017, when temperatures were high, than in June of 2016. In addition to increasing consumer costs, the increased use of electricity, as well as the increased temperature of air and water, contribute to more power outages. These outages impose costs not only on power companies but also on the business that find themselves without electricity. According to the World Bank, in 2017 the lost value, worldwide, due to electrical outages reached 4.64% of the sales of the affected firms (but WB does not provide the value of these sales).

Several studies estimate the costs of power outages due to extreme weather (heat, cold, hurricanes and other storms) from a low of 0.016% of GDP for the US to a medium 0.083% for Italy to a high of 1.7% for Bangladesh. Using the average of these estimates (0.025% of GDP) and applying it to the 2050 GNE we get the following costs for outages: $46.5 billion under Scenario 1, and $195.8 billion under Scenario 2 (in 2010 US dollars). Note that these costs include all types of outages due to weather and not just heat-related outages.

c) Finally, some professions cannot use air conditioning to comfort themselves (e.g., construction workers) during heatwaves. As such, they stop working with negative consequences for a country's economic output. In addition, people are generally less productive during extreme heat. One just needs to look at the GDP data for northern and southern countries to see that this is generally true. And this is so, not because the citizens of the northern countries are more productive or have a better work ethic, but simply because in the south it is hotter and as such harder to perform efficiently. Studies have found that for every 1° Celsius above room temperature, labour productivity declines by 0.33% to 2.0%[34].

A study, by the London School of Economics[35], on the impact of heatwaves on labour productivity estimated it to be 0.4% of London's GDP, while another study in Australia estimated it to be between 0.33% and 0.47% of Australia's GDP[36].

So, using the 0.4% figure as the costs of lost output and applying it to our projected GNE in 2050 (in 2010 US$), we get, a cost estimate of US$743 billion under Scenario 1, and US$3.14 trillion under Scenario 2. This is again a conservative estimate as a study for the city of Nanjing found this impact to be 3.43% of the city's GDP[37].

Apart from the above direct impacts of heat on humans, excessive heat also has indirect impacts. According to WHO, pollen and other aeroallergens are also higher in extreme heat. These can trigger asthma, which affects around 235 million people[38], 383,00 of which died in 2015. Most of these deaths (80%) occurred in low-income and lower-middle-income countries as treatment in those countries is lacking.

A study in the US[39] estimated that 15.4 million people had treated-asthma and that the total annual costs for asthma in the US, including

---

[34] "Effects of Heat Stress on Construction Labor Productivity in Hong Kong: A Case Study of Rebar Workers", Wen Yi and Albert P. C. Chan, Int J Environ Res Public Health. 2017 Sep; 14(9): 1055. And "The Labor Productivity Impacts of Climate Change: Implications for Global Poverty", Jisung Park, World Bank Climate Change and Poverty Conference, 2015.

[35] "Heat waves, productivity, and the urban economy: What are the costs?", LSE, Grantham Research Institute on Climate Change and the Environment, July 2016.

[36] "Heat Stress Causes Substantial Labour Productivity Loss in Australia", Kerstin K. Zander, Wouter J. W. Botzen, Elspeth Oppermann, Tord Kjellstrom & Stephen T. Garnett, Nature Climate Change volume 5, pages 647–651 (2015).

[37] "Assessment of the Economic Impacts of Heat Waves: A Case Study of Nanjing, China", Yang Xia, Yuan Li, Dabo Guan, David Mendoza Tinoco, Journal of Cleaner Production 171 · October 2017.

[38] WHO, Asthma Facts.

[39] Tursynbek Nurmagambetov, Robin Kuwahara, Paul Garbe: The Economic Burden of Asthma in the United States, 2008 -2013. *Annals of the American Thoracic Society*, 2018.

medical care, absenteeism, and mortality, was US$81.9 billion in 2015 dollars.

According to the Global Asthma Report[40], in 2016 asthma contributed 23.7 million DALYS (disability-adjusted life years) globally (indirect costs), while its direct costs (medical care) vary from a low of US$150 per patient in Abu Dhabi to a high of US$3,000 in the US. Here we used US$3,000 per patient for North America and Australia, US$839 for Europe (based on a Finish study) and US$150 for everyone else.

If the increase, between 2015 and 2050, in asthma sufferers worldwide is proportional to the increase in temperature then in 2050 there will be 428.7 million asthma sufferers under Scenario 1 (194 million additional), of which 699,132 will die annually (316,132 additional), while under Scenario 2, there will be 2.8 billion asthma sufferers (2.6 billion additional), of which 4,548,562 will die annually (4,165,562 additional).

As for the direct costs of these additional asthma sufferers, under Scenario 1 they will reach US$152 billion, while under Scenario 2 they will reach US$2.3 trillion (in 2016 dollars). The additional indirect costs will be US$199.6 billion under Scenario 1 and US$2.98 trillion under Scenario 2. So, the total direct and indirect additional costs will be US$351.3 billion under Scenario 1 and US$5.25 trillion under Scenario 2.

∽⑨ॐ☯②

But we are not done yet with the impacts of increased temperatures. Vector and waterborne diseases, such as malaria, dengue and cholera are also facilitated by increasing temperatures and changing rainfall patterns. Rising freshwater temperatures are likely to increase the prevalence of harmful algae, pathogens and bacteria and therefore are likely to affect humans who are using these waters for recreation (swimming), bathing and drinking as well as for food production.

Table 13 shows our estimates[41] of the increased number of infections for three of these waterborne diseases and the associated economic costs.

The number of infections and deaths increases by 40.6% under Scenario 1 and by 203% under Scenario 2, while the associated economic costs

---

[40] Global Asthma Report, 2018, Global Asthma Network.

[41] The projections are based on the following equation:
(Number of infections) = 96,364,612 + 59,100,655*(Temperature change) + 0.021259*(Population). This equation has an $R^2 = 74\%$.

increase by 45% and 212%, respectively. The economic costs include direct costs for treating those infected, as well as indirect costs such as loss of productivity and the value of human life.

	# of malaria, dengue, and cholera annual infections	Direct and indirect annual economic costs 2016 US$ billions	Number of annual deaths
Table 13: Malaria, dengue, and cholera			
Scenario 1 (temp. changes by 2.46°C in 2050)			
2016	318,857,716	53.3	3,611,102
2050	449,378,178	77.4	5,089,261
Scenario 2 (temp. changes by 11.2°C in 2050)			
2016	318,857,716	53.3	3,611,102
2050	966,162,444	166.4	10,941,904
Source: for malaria cases and deaths, IHME; for dengue "The Global Burden of Dengue: an analysis from the Global Burden of Disease Study 2013", J. Stanaway et all, PMC; for cholera, WHO; for 2016 economic costs WHO and CDC; the 2050 projections are my estimates			

b. **Droughts and wildfires**: Although the data on the number of droughts do not exhibit any discernible trend overall at the global level, water loss due to evaporation is bound to increase with higher temperatures and hence result, locally, in more frequent, more severe, and longer droughts. In terms of the earth's area covered by droughts (excluding deserts and ice sheets), the average from 1950 to 2017, for all types of drought, shows no change at around 26% of the planet's surface, while severe droughts (about 9%) and extreme droughts (about 3%) show a small increase after 1984. So, although the overall number of droughts is not increasing, the impacts in terms of costs are increasing due to the increase in their severity.

Africa accounts for the largest number of droughts (41%), while North America accounts for the largest number of wildfires.

Unfortunately, only a few countries have consistent and reliable time series data that one could use to estimate the relationship between the costs of droughts and wildfires and climate change (namely, only the US). According to CRED[42], between 2006 and 2016 there were 264 drought events worldwide that, in 2016, affected 393 million people and caused, for the whole period, US$81.3 billion in damages, or an average of US$7.4 billion per year. For wildfires, there were 100 events that

---

[42] Annual Disaster Statistical Review, 2016.

affected 158,000 people in 2016 and caused, for the whole period, US$29.3 billion in damages or an average of US$2.7 billion per year.

As was the case with heatwaves, CRED's estimates are way off the mark. According to the US National Oceanic and Atmospheric Administration[43] (NOAA), between 2006 and 2016 there were 10 drought events in the US that caused US$95.7 billion in damages or an average of US$8.7 billion per year, and 8 wildfire events that caused US$17.7 billion in damages, or an average of US$1.6 billion per year (all numbers are inflation adjusted).

Although the US data on wildfires could be compatible with CRED's, the data regarding the economic damages of droughts are not – the US total exceeds CRED's estimate of the world total! To make CRED's total for droughts compatible to NOAA's numbers we need to add US$3.5 billion for 2016 and US$58.5 billion for the period 2006-2015 (CRED's average for the period is $3.35 billion for North America while NOAA's numbers show an average of $9.2 billion for the US alone). So, the world-wide damages from droughts and wildfires for the period 2006-2016 is US$172.6 billion.

Assuming a proportional relationship between temperature and economic damages due to droughts and wildfires, the annual damages under Scenario 1 could reach US$42.9 billion, while under Scenario 2 they could reach US$195.3 billion, or US$1.95 trillion for the 2040-2050 decade (in 2016 US$) – that is 1.1 times greater than the GDP of Sub-Saharan Africa in 2017 (in 2010 US$)!

c. **Heavy downpours, floods, and landslides**: I have included heavy downpours, defined as 100 mm or more of rain over a period of 24 hours, and floods in one section because they are related and as such easier to calculate. But floods are caused, or amplified by both, weather and human-related factors. Major weather factors include heavy or prolonged precipitation, snowmelt, thunderstorms, storm surges from hurricanes, and ice or debris jams. Human factors include structural failures of dams and levees, altered drainage, and alterations in land-cover (such as pavements and roads).

"There is now medium confidence that human-induced greenhouse gases have contributed to changes in heavy precipitation events at the global scale. We show that over the last three decades the number of record-breaking events has significantly increased in the global mean.

---

[43] Billion-Dollar Weather and Climate Disasters, NOAA.

Globally, this increase has led to 12 % more record-breaking rainfall events over (the average of) *1981–2010."*[44]. This study also indicates that the impacts vary significantly from region to region. In South East Asia the record-breaking rainfall events are now 56% higher, in Europe 31% higher, and in the central US 24% higher than the reference period. In contrast, some regions experienced a significant decrease in record-breaking daily rainfall events. In the Mediterranean, the reduction is 27%, and in the western US is 21%, exposing both regions to risks of severe droughts.

Again, as with previous impacts of climate change, poor countries suffer more than rich countries.

What kind of problems heavy rainfalls create?
- They cause flooding which kills people and damages buildings, infrastructure, crops, and livestock;
- They cause landslides, which also kill people, disrupt transport and communications, and cause damage to buildings and infrastructure;
- By overloading of sewage systems and water treatment facilities they increase the risk of waterborne diseases when untreated sewage and agricultural runoff water is discharged into water bodies;

According to CRED, in 2016 there were **164 floods and 13 landslides** world-wide – higher than the average of the previous 9 years. "*The two countries most hit by floods were China (13) and Indonesia (10) and these numbers of occurrence remained, for both countries, above their 2006-2015 annual average (10.7 and 7.7, respectively). In 2016, four countries experienced a number of hydrological disasters unexpectedly high compared to their 2006-2015 annual average: the six floods in 2016 in Haiti represent 3 times their annual average and four floods reported, each, in Malaysia and Angola amounted to twice their annual average. Inversely, the only flood which occurred in the Philippines in 2016 represents a decrease of 88% compared to the 2006-2015 annual average and, in Brazil, the two floods of 2016 a decrease of 60%.*" (CRED, 2016)

The total number of deaths due to floods and landslides reached 5,092 in 2016, below the average annual of 6,657 of the previous 9 years. The **total number of people affected by floods, heavy downpours, and landslides in 2016 reached 78.1 million**, slightly below its 2006-2015

---

[44] "Increased Record-breaking Precipitation Events Under Global Warming", Jascha Lehmann, Dim Coumou, Katja Frieler, 2015, Climatic Change, 132(4), 501-515.

annual average (82.6 million). Most of the countries affected were in Africa and Asia.

In 2016, flood damages amounted to US$60.3 billion (I have added US$1.3 billion to the CRED figure to match the 2016 US data reported by NOAA), and for the decade 2006-2016 amounted to US$365.5 billion. However, in 2016 only 31 of the 79 countries that experienced hydrological disasters reported their damages, which means that the 2016 economic costs of floods could be as high as US$153.7 billion and the total for the decade could be US$458.9 billion, if there is no underreporting in the previous years – which is probably not true.

Again, due to lack of annual data at the world level, we cannot properly estimate the relationship between economic damages from floods and temperature increases. Instead, we have to assume a proportional relationship. So, under Scenario 1 the damages due to floods will reach US$114 billion per year, while under Scenario 2 they will reach US$519 billion per year or US$5.2 trillion for the 2040-2050 decade – that is equal to the combined GDP of Africa and the Middle East in 2017 (in 2010 US$).

d. **Hurricanes**: As the graph below shows, although the number of hurricanes of category 3, 4 and 5 has been increasing since 1960, this is not true for other types of tropical storms.

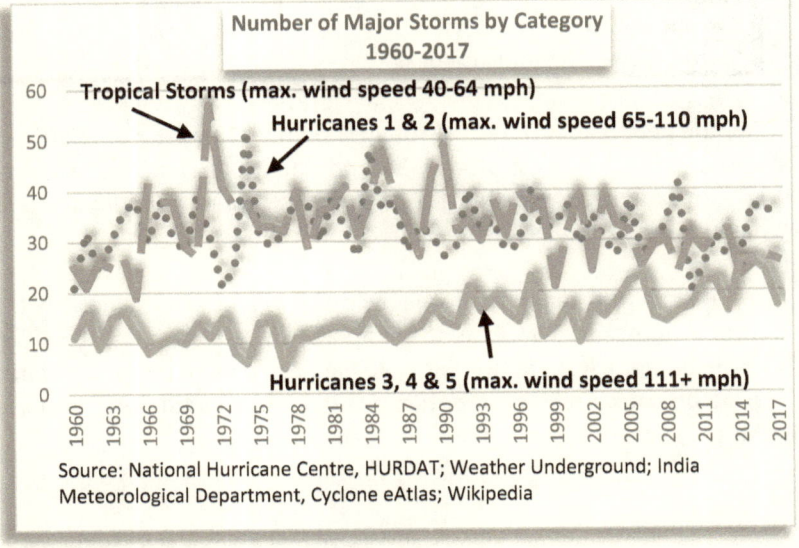

The average number of tropical storms and hurricanes of category 1 and 2 has been declining from decade to decade after their peak during the 1987-1990 period – maybe there is a fixed number of hurricanes that can form within a season, implying that when one type increases, the other must decline. In any case, it is the hurricanes of categories 3, 4 and 5 that create extensive damages and kill people.

For North America, where data are available thanks, again, to US agencies, the average annual economic damages have been increasing substantially as Table 14 shows.

Table 14: Average Annual Economic Damages from Tropical Storms				
	In the North Atlantic		In the World	
Decade	$Billions adjusted by CPI to 2017	# of Hurricanes 3, 4 or 5	$Billions adjusted by CPI to 2017	# of Hurricanes 3, 4 or 5
1960s Average annual	3.3 0.33	7.1 0.71		11.8 1.18
1970s Average annual	4.2 0.42	7.2 0.72		10.9 1.09
1980s Average annual	5.6 0.56	6.9 0.69		13.0 1.30
1990s Average annual	10.3 1.03	7.7 0.77		16.0 1.60
2000s Average annual	38.4 3.84	10.2 1.02		16.7 1.67
2010-2017 Average annual	51.2 7.31	9.3 1.33	67.8 9.68	21.3 3.04
Source: NOAA; Weather Underground				

For the period 2010-2017 the total economic damages from hurricanes, cyclones and tropical storms around the world reached an annual average of US$67.8 billion (in 2017 prices), while the annual average number of deaths reached 2,812.

What does the temperature have to do with the formation of these strong hurricanes? Well, as the graph below shows, a lot. Again, one could argue that these two lines just happen to trend upward and hence have no causal relationship, but meteorologists argue that hurricanes form because the surface of the ocean warms up.

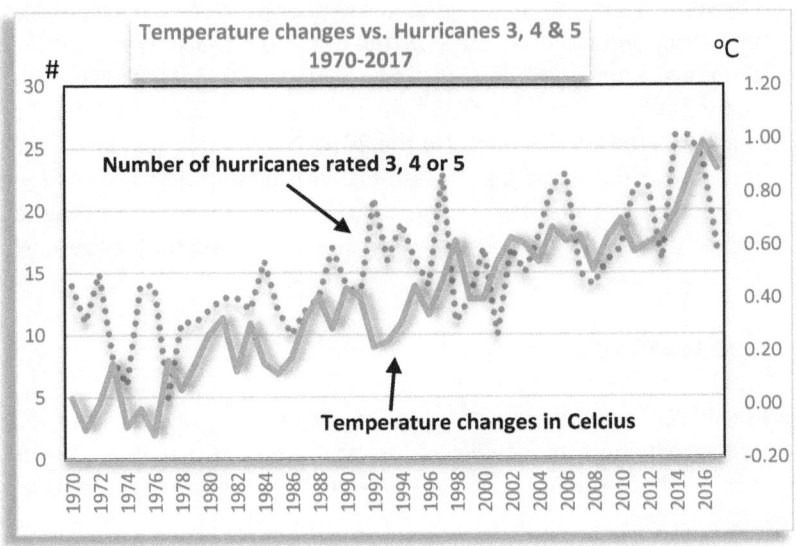

Based on these data, we are able to predict[45] that under Scenario 1, the average annual number of hurricanes rated 3, 4 or 5 will increase to 32.3 during the 2040-2050 decade – a 52% increase over their number during the 2010-2017 period – while under Scenario 2, the average annual number of hurricanes rated 3, 4 or 5 will reach 36 – a 70% increase over their number during the 2010-2017 period. In effect under Scenario 2, the South-East region of the US, the Caribbean, South Asia, Northern Australia, and Southeast Asia may become inhabitable, at least during hurricane season!

If the relationship between economic damages and the number of hurricanes rated 3, 4 or 5 is linear then the average annual costs for the 2040-2050 period will be US$103 billion, under Scenario 1, and US$115 billion under Scenario 2. Some other significant costs, such as imposing new building codes on new buildings, are not included here.

e. **Other Storms:** These storms include thunderstorms, tornados, hail storms, winter storms, and freezes. Although the climate change

---

[45] I used the S-curve to estimate the number of hurricanes (because hurricanes cannot go on increasing indefinitely): $PPH = 25.6/(1+e^{-x})$, where x is the annual temperature change and PPH is the Preliminary Predicted Hurricanes. The difference between PPH and the actual number of hurricanes in every year produces a series of numbers that were then fitted using a time series regression. The parameters of the time series regression were then used to multiply PPH to obtain the predicted number of hurricanes. The number 25.6 is the average that will make the number of hurricanes in every year equal to the value computed by using the S-curve $1/(1+e^{x})$.

literature seems to imply that these storms have also increased in frequency and severity in the US, the data from NOAA show no trend in thunderstorms or tornadoes from 1960 to 2017. However, data on economic damages in the US[46] do show a trend from US$2.6 billion in the 1980s to US$16.9 billion in the 2010-2017 period (adjusted to 2018 prices). But this could be the result of just missing data in earlier years. As such we will not include the costs of such storm systems, although some of their effects have already been captured under the costs of electrical outages and flooding.

3) Sea level rise

The rise in sea level has the potential to eclipse any other climate related socio-economic impacts. Sea levels rise because of two reasons: a) the ice sheets over land are melting and b) the oceanic water is expanding as it gets warmer.

Over the years when data are available, sea levels not only increased but, recently, they increased at an increasing rate: the average annual rate of change in the sea level for each decade prior to 2000 was 0.57 inches, while during the 2000s and 2010s it rose to 0.95 inches. There is a high level of agreement amongst scientists[47] that by the year 2100 the sea level will rise between 8 inches and 6.6 feet (0.2 meters to 2 meters) – a prediction that seems to have a ridiculously large range.

As the graph below shows, the sea level in 2015 was already 8.9 inches higher than it was in 1880 – that is, it is already higher than what the scientists have claimed to be the lower bound of its rise in 2100! It also shows that it correlates nicely with temperature changes.

In 2010, based on data published by the World Bank[48], 5% of the world's population and 1.1% of its landmass lied in areas where the elevation was less than 5 meters from sea level. For East Asia and the Pacific and for the Middle East and North Africa the proportion of the population living at elevations of less than 5 meters is 8.3% and 7.1%, respectively, meaning these regions will suffer more than others.

---

[46] NOAA, National Centers for Environmental Information: U.S. Billion-Dollar Weather and Climate Disasters, 2018.

[47] NOAA, Climate.gov

[48] The World Bank, World Development Indicators: Climate variability, exposure to impact and resilience.

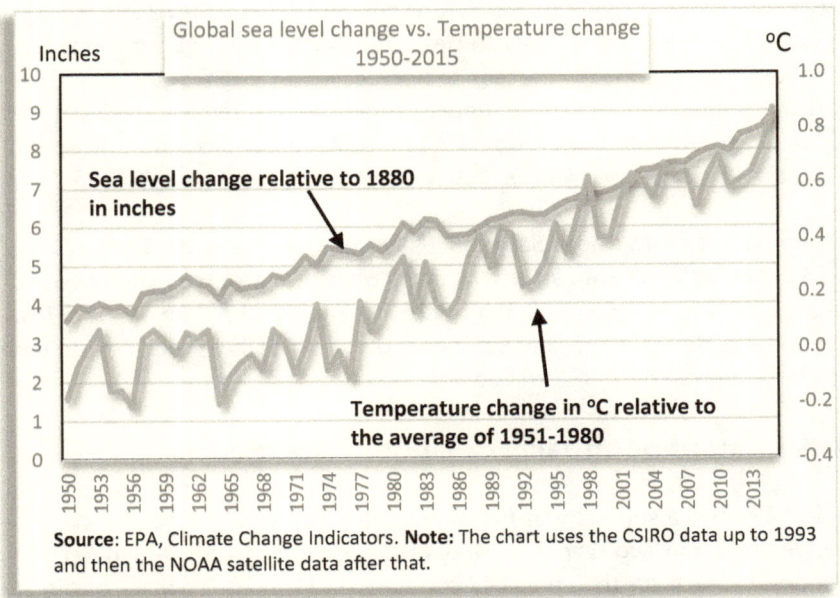

Source: EPA, Climate Change Indicators. Note: The chart uses the CSIRO data up to 1993 and then the NOAA satellite data after that.

At the world level, 5% of its population translates to 693 million people in 2010 and 977 million people in 2050 being at risk and hence prone to mass migrations. These migrations are bound to increase conflicts in regions with existing environmental problems, like the Middle East, South Asia, and Africa. If the world had problems accommodating four million Syrian refugees in 2017, how would it cope with almost a billion of them?

When the sea level rises, the world has two options: do nothing and let all the low-lying countries flood, or protect them, as they do in the Netherlands, with sea dikes. The costs of doing nothing is difficult to estimate as it needs an inventory of all the things that will be flooded. On the other hand, estimating the costs of seas dikes is easier. And if we assume that the costs of building sea dikes to be less than or equal to the economic benefits of doing so, then these costs can be considered as the lower-bound costs of the sea level rise.

The costs of building sea dikes, and other river protection structures, around the world are estimated globally at US$7.7 trillion for every 0.4 meters (15.7 inches) of sea level rise and US$9.6 trillion for every 0.63 meters (24.8 inches) of sea level rise[49] (it includes capital and maintenance costs).

---

[49] "Global Investment Costs for Coastal Defence Through the 21st Century", Robert J. Nicholls, Daniel Lincke, Jochen Hinkel and Thomas van der Pol, published in the Global Climate Forum.

Instead of using the NOAA-mentioned estimates of the sea level rise in 2100, we will estimate what it is likely to be in 2050 under our two scenarios. We estimate[50] that for every increase in temperature by 1 degree Celsius, the sea level will rise by 4.69 inches. So, under Scenario 1, the sea level in 2050 will be 16.3 inches higher than it was in 1880, while under Scenario 2 it will be 57.3 inches higher, or 4.8 feet or 1.46 meters.

What would it cost? Under Scenario 1 the costs, at the world level, will be US$8 trillion by 2050, with an annual maintenance costs after that of US$800 billion, while under Scenario 2, the costs will be US$22.2 trillion – that is 18% bigger than the GDP of the European Union in 2017 - with an annual maintenance cost of US$2.2 trillion after that.

4) Summary of impacts of climate change

Table 15 shows a summary of the human and economic impacts of climate change under our two scenarios. Under Scenario 1, the world would need to spend $1 billion more than the 2017 combined GDP (in 2010 dollars) of Africa, the Middle East and Latin America & the Caribbean to compensate for the annual costs of climate change, while under Scenario 2, it will need to spend US$41 trillion which is US$2 trillion more than the combined GDP in 2017 (in 2010 dollars) of North America and the European Union!

As for the dead, under Scenario 1 we will be losing a bit more than one Guinea per year, while under Scenario 2 a bit more than one Iraq. In fact, under Scenario 2, the annual deaths by 2050 will account for 0.4% of the world's population and 73% of its annual growth - which means that the world population cannot increase as forecasted.

It appears then, that neither Scenario 1, nor Scenario 2 are achievable from a climate change perspective and in fact, both scenarios will make everyone worse off, especially those we were trying to help – i.e., the poor countries.

Our estimates here are very conservative for three reasons (we have not included these impacts because of lack of data):

A) As temperatures increase, the methane stored in permafrost regions of the Arctic will be released. Remember that methane is at least 20 times more potent a greenhouse gas than CO_2. There are some estimates that by 2100, one gigaton of methane (an amount equal to 35% of the

---

[50] The equation that describes the relationship between temperature and sea level is this: (Sea level) = 4.75 + 4.69*(Temperature change). This equation has an R^2=88%.

methane level in 2008) and 37 gigatons of carbon dioxide could be released from permafrost soils[51].

Table 15: Summary of Annual Economic and Human Impacts of Climate Change by 2050

	Scenario 1		Scenario 2	
	Deaths/ extinctions	Economic loss $Trillions	Deaths/ extinctions	Economic loss $Trillions
Extinctions and deaths due to food shortages	99% of mammal species 47% of fish species 6.3% of plant species 39.3% of bird species 10,000,000 people	$4.000	All mammal species All fish species 50% of plant species All bird species 23,200,000 people	$9.300
Heatwaves - Direct - Communicable diseases - Asthma	1,005,429 1,478,159 316,132	$0.793 $0.0241 $0.3513	2,987,495 7,330,802 4,165,562	$3.345 $0.1131 $5.2500
Droughts	Captured under extinctions	$0.0429	Captured under extinctions	$0.1953
Heavy rains, Floods & Landslides	8,697	$0.114	31,160	$0.519
Hurricanes	4,000	$0.103	4,886	$0.115
Sea level rise	No direct deaths are anticipated	$8.000	No direct deaths are anticipated	$22.200
TOTAL	12,812,417	$13.4283	37,719,905	$41.0324

If these estimates are correct, then by 2050 we would expect another 19 billion tonnes of CO_2 equivalent gasses (half of the estimate for 2100) to be added to the atmosphere. This will increase the 2050 temperature under Scenario 1 to 3°C (a 22.5% increase over the temperature we used in our calculations this far) and under Scenario 2 to 11.74°C (a 4.8% increase). As such, the impacts under Scenario 1 could increase to 15.7 million deaths and $16.4 trillion of economic damages, while under

---

[51] Knoblauch C, Beer C, Liebner S, Grigoriev M N, Pfeiffer E-M (2018): Methane production as key to the greenhouse gas budget of thawing permafrost; Nature Climate Change, DOI: 10.1038/s41558-018-0095-z.

Scenario 2 they could increase to 39.5 million deaths and $43 trillion of economic damages.

B) The unfreezing of permafrost could also release viruses which could greatly contribute to more deaths and sickness[52] (data on this issue are impossible to gather since the existence of these viruses is circumstantial). For example, in the summer of 2016, and following a heatwave that raised the temperatures in Siberia to 35°C, there was an outbreak of anthrax that killed a boy and 2,300 reindeer.

C) Many of the world's nuclear plants are aging and scheduled to be retired. Since there are practically no new developments in nuclear power plants underway, they are likely to be replaced by coal or natural gas plants, thus increasing CO_2 and PM2.5 emissions[53]. A recent report[54] by the Union of Concerned Scientists estimates that in the United States, more than one-third of its nuclear plants are unprofitable and scheduled to be replaced by coal or natural gas plants.

Water

We have discussed already the impact of climate change on water quality. But water quality and quantity are not only affected by climate change. The number of people and industries using water, and the way they use it, affects its quantity and quality.

Water Quantity

Total water withdrawals (by consumers, industry, and agriculture) increased by 50% between 1972 and 2014 which resulted in an increase in the proportion of renewable water resources being withdrawn from 5.1% to 7.7. And because the total amount of renewable water resources in the world is fixed, the annual water resources available per capita declined from 14,212 m^3 in 1972 to 7,500 m^3 in 2014. This may not sound serious at the world level, but in 2014 there were 15 countries (out of 186 with data) using more than 100% of their available water resources and accounting for 258 million people, or 3.5% of the world's population.

---

[52] "There are Diseases Hidden in Ice and are Walking Up", the BBC, May 4, 2017.
[53] Power plants are the largest contributors of greenhouse gas emissions.
[54] "The Nuclear Power Dilemma", (2018).

How could a country consume more water than it has? Well, the total available renewable water resources include internal and external, to a country, surface and ground water. It does not include re-using treated (or untreated) municipal wastewater and re-using (untreated) agricultural drainage water and nor does it include desalination – which creates its own problems as it requires huge amounts of energy and hence produces greenhouse gas emissions. As such, those that need more water than what is available to them will either have to recycle it or produce it from the ocean.

In 2014, agriculture used most (70%) of the renewable water resources. This ratio was up from 67% in 1972, which makes intuitive sense as more people need more food, and more food production requires more water.

So, how do the water-related problems look like under our two scenarios? Under Scenario 1, water withdrawals will reach 12.3 trillion cubic meters by 2050. This accounts for 22% of the available water resources. Out of 186 countries with water data, 38 will use more than 100% of their available resources – up from the 15 countries in 2014. These countries will account for 2.9 billion people or 30% of the world's population in 2050. Furthermore, seven of these countries, accounting for 86 million people, are landlocked and as such cannot use the desalination option.

Under Scenario 2, water withdrawals will reach 147 trillion cubic meters which is almost three times greater than the total available water resources of the world! And if this is not bad enough at the world level, at the country level there will now be 97 (out of 186) countries consuming more than 100% of their renewable water resources accounting for 7.4 billion people or 76% of the world's population in 2050 – creating even more opportunities for local conflicts and mass migrations.

Now if you are thinking that desalination would solve their problem, out of these 97 countries, 23, accounting for 883 million people, are landlocked. As such this option is not available to them. They could use water recycling, but recycling has its limitations. Or they could migrate to another country that has no water problems. But 883 million people – this is the minimum number at risk of migration; the maximum could be as high as 7.4 billion – are a lot of people and it is hard to see how a country or a group of countries could accommodate them (almost three times the population of the United States).

How much would water recycling and desalination cost? If the countries that will consume more than their available water resources use, on average, a combination of desalination and water recycling (half and half), we get US$1.8 trillion for Scenario 1 and US$107.8 trillion for Scenario 2[55].

So, from a water resource perspective, Scenario 2, is not feasible. But Scenario 1 is not much of an option either from an economic perspective ($1.8 trillion is bigger than the GDP of Sub-Saharan Africa) or from a technical perspective for the seven landlocked countries.

The above discussion points to another factor that is missing from our estimates of greenhouse gas emissions for 2050. That is, our estimates do not contain the full impact on emissions from increased desalination[56]. The impact that is included in our estimates is limited to the level of desalination already in place up to 2012. But this level must increase dramatically in order to accommodate the world's water needs by 2050.

I estimate that under Scenario 1 the increased desalination in 2050 by those in short supply of fresh water will add another 10.6 billion tonnes of greenhouse gasses, or about 9% to the estimate we have used in this report, and 521 billion tonnes under Scenario 2, or 124% more than the estimate we used here! These increased levels of greenhouse gas emissions will increase the temperature in 2050 by another 0.3° C under Scenario 1 and by 14.2° C under Scenario 2. In other words, the temperature increase in 2050 under Scenario 1 will be 2.8 °C above the reference period, while under Scenario 2 it will be 25.4 ° C higher – in effect, more than doubling our estimated temperature in 2050! I have not incorporated these emissions into my main estimates because I do not know how people will react to the lack of water. For example, they could just migrate to other countries that are not faced with this problem, thus adding to problems associated with migration and local conflicts.

Water Quality

We discussed earlier how floods can overwhelm municipal treatment facilities and cause them to discharge untreated water into water bodies. Unfortunately, data on the quality of fresh water are very sparse. From what we have, Table 16 presents a limited, but depressing picture.

---

[55] Although recycling is cheaper than desalination, it requires the presence of sewage systems, which many countries do not have. For unit costs, we used $1.5 per 1,000 gallons of water for recycling and $5 for desalination from the report "Desalination and Water Recycling", Mission 2017.

[56] Reverse osmosis is estimated to produce 0.4-6.7 kilos of greenhouse gasses per m³ of water: "Carbon footprint of water reuse and desalination: a review of greenhouse gas emissions and estimation tools", P. K. Cornejo, M. V. E. Santana, D. R. Hokanson, J. R. Mihelcic and Qiong Zhang, Journal of Ware Reuse and Desalination, 2014.

Table 16: Water Quality in the EU					
The Number of Rivers & Lakes in the European Union having Ecological Status:					
High	Good	Moderate	Poor	Bad	Unknown
6,828	25,797	35,702	11,657	5,344	3,906
Number of Rivers & Lakes in the EU having Chemical Status:			# of Transitional & Coastal Waters in the EU having Chemical Status:		
Good	Failing to be good	Unknown	Good	Failing to be good	Unknown
40,064	49,929	17,386	1,995	1,149	473
EU's Ground Water having a Chemical Status (km^2):			% of EU's Ground Water experiencing:		
Good	Poor	Unknown	Chemical, nutrient, organic, microbiol. pollution		Some other problem
3,201,133	1,088,402	41,476	44%		20%
Source: European Environment Agency (EEA)					

Of the European Union's lakes and rivers, 62% have a moderate to bad ecological status, and 55% have a "failing to be good" chemical status[57]. Of its transitional[58] and coastal waters, 37% failed to be good. Finally, 25% of its groundwater is in poor chemical status.

For Latin America, 36-40% of river stretches are moderately to severely polluted by faecal coliform bacteria (human and animal faeces), while in Africa this percentage is between 26-37% and in Asia it is between 44-65%[59] (Table 17).

Organic pollution affects 9-15% of the river stretches in Latin America, 10-19% of those in Africa and 15-22% of those in Asia. Finally, salinity affects 3.4-

---

[57] These are the definitions provided by the EEA: "Ecological status is an assessment of the quality of the structure and functioning of surface water ecosystems. It shows the influence of pressures (e.g. pollution and habitat degradation) on the identified quality elements. Ecological status is determined for each of the surface water bodies of rivers, lakes, transitional waters, and coastal waters, based on biological quality elements and supported by physicochemical and hydro-morphological quality elements. For surface waters, good chemical status means that no concentrations of priority substances exceed the relevant Environmental Quality Standards established in the Directive 2008/105/EC. EQS aim to protect the most sensitive species from direct toxicity, including predators and humans via secondary poisoning. A smaller group of priority hazardous substances were identified in the Priority Substances Directive as uPBT (ubiquitous -present, appearing or found everywhere - persistent, bioaccumulative and toxic). The uPBTs are mercury, brominated diphenyl ethers (pBDE), tributyltin and certain polyaromatic hydrocarbons (PAHs)".

[58] Transitional waters are the ones at rivers' deltas.

[59] UNEP 2016, A Snapshot of the World's Water Quality: Towards a Global Assessment.

4.9% of the river stretches in Latin America, 7-12% in Africa, and 7-14% in Asia.

In general, European rivers and lakes seem to suffer mainly from industrial and agricultural pollution, while African, Latin America, and Asian rivers suffer mainly from bacterial pollution stemming from the dumping of human and animal faeces untreated into them.

Faecal coliform pollution is likely to get worse in the future as the world's population and food production increase. But so will chemical pollution as more people require more food and more stuff; and agriculture and industry are major polluters of rivers and lakes. And since population growth will increase the most in Asia and Africa, water quality is bound to get worse there.

Table 17: Percentage of river stretches (km) by class of pollution Minimum and maximum monthly values over the 2008-2010 period			
	Latin America	Africa	Asia
Water Pollution class: Faecal coliform pollution			
Low pollution	60%-65%	63%-74%	35%-56%
Moderate pollution	13%	13%-14%	13%-15%
Severe pollution	22%-27%	13%-23%	31%-50%
Water Pollution class: Organic pollution (Dissolved Oxygen, Biochemical Oxygen Demand, Ammonia, Chloride, pH level)			
Low pollution	86%-91%	81%-89%	78%-85%
Moderate pollution	3%-4%	3%-4%	4%-5%
Severe pollution	6%-10%	7%-15%	11%-17%
Water Pollution class: Salinity			
Low pollution	95%-96%	87%-93%	86%-93%
Moderate pollution	3%-4%	5%-7%	5%-10%
Severe pollution	0.4%-0.9%	2%-5%	2%-4%
Source: A Snapshot of the World's Water Quality, UNEP report, 2016			

Although the above data provide a rather depressing picture of the quality of fresh water, they do not allow us to calculate the economic and human costs of water pollution.

The problem with severe faecal coliform pollution is that one needs not drink the water in order to get sick – you can get sick by bathing, swimming, breathing water spray, or by eating vegetables that have been irrigated or washed with contaminated water. Since we do not have any data on infections while bathing or swimming, or eating contaminated food, we will concentrate on drinking under the understanding that this underestimates the infections and the costs.

According to the World Bank (with some estimates of missing values made by myself), in 2015, 53% of the world population had access to "safely managed drinking water services" – meaning 47% did not. Further, the number of deaths in 2016 due to diarrhea disease contracted through, mainly, drinking or bathing in contaminated water reached 871,394 or 11.7 people per 100,000 population. If the situation continues (and there is no reason why it should not, given our history up to now), then by 2050 there will be 1,589,107 deaths due to diarrhea (other diseases contracted through contaminated water were dealt with in the previous section).

In addition to killing people, diarrhea makes those it does not kill sick and hence withdraws them, temporarily, from the workforce. According to WHO, "every year diarrhoea kills 525,000 children under five. Globally, there are 1.7 billion cases of childhood diarrhoeal disease every year". As such, in 2016 there were 346,394 non-childhood deaths due to diarrhea and using the same incidence of death among children infected with diarrhea we get a total of 1.1 billion adults infected with diarrhea.

We estimate, then, that in 2050 there will be 2 billion adult sufferers of diarrhea. Assuming the average length of infliction to be three days, the world will lose 1.15% of the available work days per year. Using the average per capita income by country, we get a total economic loss of US$39.3 billion without counting the dead or medical costs.

Of course, polluted water does not only give one bacterial diarrhea. It could also contribute to long-term health problems, or death, if it contains toxins. However, there are no data we can use to estimate these deaths. The only thing we can say here is that almost half (47%) of the world's population does not have access to safe drinking water and as such is at risk of developing acute and/or chronic diseases.

∽⑨≈ಌ②

Another problem that the pervasive presence of humans creates is the production of large amounts of garbage that pollute our oceans. According to UNESCO, agricultural runoffs, pesticides, coastal tourism, port and harbour developments, damming of rivers, urban development, mining, aquaculture, untreated sewer, and manufacturing, among others, account for 80% of marine pollution globally. Untreated sewage and agricultural runoffs have contributed to low oxygen areas in the oceans, called dead zones, where marine life cannot survive due to lack of dissolved oxygen (the bacteria eat it). Presently there are 500 dead zones covering 245,000 km^2 globally – an area equal to the surface area of the UK.

According to the UN Environment Agency, in 2006 every square mile of the ocean contained 46,000 pieces of floating plastic. A UNEP study estimates the economic impact of plastic in the marine environment to be US$13 billion (this includes impacts on fisheries, tourism, and cleaning beaches) [60].

Since the garbage we generate is proportional to how many of us there are and how much we consume, by 2050 the dead zones under Scenario 1 will cover 765,852 km^2 of the ocean, while under Scenario 2, will cover 3,231,915 km^2 – that is the surface area of India!

As for the pieces of plastic per square mile, under Scenario 1 there will be 144,000 of them, while under Scenario 2 there will be 607,000 – in other words in every 4 square meters of the entire ocean surface, there will be one piece of plastic floating – I wonder if our planet will still look blue from space.

The costs under Scenario 1 of oceanic pollution will reach US$33 billion, while under Scenario 2 they will reach US$140 billion.

Of course, these estimates could underestimate the costs because pollution could have an all-or-nothing impact, rather than a continuous marginal impact on some industries. For example, people usually go to sun destinations to primarily enjoy the beach and not to sleep in a bed where one million other people slept or to watch hotel staff clean the beaches. The Caribbean tourism industry alone is valued at US$30 billion, that of the European part of the Mediterranean at US$175 billion, North Africa at US$9 billion, Indonesia and Thailand US$61 billion, Hawaii and the Pacific Islands US$17 billion and Central America at US$12 billion (UNWTO, 2016). If all this primarily beach tourism is threatened, a total of US$304 billion may be a memory of the past under Scenario 2 on top of the costs to the fisheries.

Air Quality

As if climate change was not enough of a deterioration in the air quality, there are some small, fine particles (less than 2.5 micrometres), that are produced by power plants, automobiles, airplanes, residential wood burning, forest fires, agricultural burning, volcanic eruptions, and sandstorms, that, because of their small size, bypass the nose and throat and penetrate deep into the lungs and the circulatory system. Studies have shown that prolong exposure to these particles cause heart and lung disease.

---

[60] Valuing Plastic, 2014.

In 2016, the global deaths due to household and ambient air pollution were 114 people per 100,000 population. Table 18 shows the distribution of deaths by region and the percent of the population in those regions that is exposed to these fine particles (called PM2.5). Except for the Middle East & North Africa, there is a linear relationship between exposure to PM2.5 and deaths – the higher the exposure, the more the deaths.

Table 18: PM2.5 Air Pollution - 2016

REGION	% of Population exposed to PM2.5 levels of air pollution exceeding WHO guidelines	Deaths per 100,000 population due to air pollution
Middle East & North Africa	100.00%	79
Sub-Saharan Africa	99.99%	187
South Asia	99.99%	179
East Asia & Pacific	98.59%	105
Europe & Central Asia	93.33%	36
Latin America & Caribbean	90.64%	39
North America	40.74%	13

Source: World Bank, World Development Indicators

Using these data, we can predict[61] that under Scenario 1, the average annual exposure in 2050 will be 65.9 micrograms per cubic meter and under Scenario 2 it will be 177.2 micrograms per cubic meter.

So, under Scenario 1, the amount of PM2.5 particles per cubic meter of air will be 559% higher than the amount recommended by WHO, which is 10 micrograms per cubic meter, and under Scenario 2 it will be 1,672% higher. As a result, deaths under Scenario 1 will reach 11,288,871 per year by 2050 and under Scenario 2, they will reach 30,345,222.

The OECD estimates that in 2015 the direct health costs associated with air pollution (PM2.5 and ground-level ozone) reached US$21 billion (in 2010 dollars) and the loss in workdays reached 1.2 billion days. The same report estimates that in 2060 the healthcare costs will rise to US$176 billion (in 2010 dollars) and the number of lost working days will rise to 3.7 billion[62].

Putting a figure on the lost work-days (using global GNE) results in a loss of US$125 billion in 2016, rising to US$304 billion in 2050 under Scenario 1

---

[61] Our equation is: (PM2.5 air pollution) = 33.28 + 0.0000000000000766*(GNE) + 7.486*(Temperature). This equation has an R^2 = 75%. Temperature enters the equation because meteorological conditions affect PM2.5 particles, and temperature affects the weather.

[62] The Economic Consequences of Outdoor Air Pollution, OECD.

(corresponding to 1.6 billion lost working days) and US$3.45 trillion under Scenario 2 (corresponding to a loss of 4.3 billion working days).

Table 19: PM2.5 air pollution, mean annual exposure (micrograms per cubic meter)							
REGION	1990	2016	% Change 2016/90	2050		Rate of Change 2050/2016	
				S. 1	S. 2	S. 1	S. 2
World	39.6	49.7	26%	65.9	177.2	33%	257%
N. America	11.0	9.0	-18%				
South Asia	60.2	77.1	28%				
L. America & Caribbean	21.0	17.8	-15%				
Europe & Central Asia	23.9	19.1	-20%				
Middle East & N. Africa	51.9	77.7	50%				
East Asia & the Pacific	38.2	42.6	12%				
Sub-Saharan Africa	60.5	77.3	28%				
Source: World Bank, World Development Indicators							

Summary of Impacts

Table 20 reproduces Table 14 with the addition of the costs associated with water and air quality and quantity.

The economic costs of Scenario 1 are now equal to 91% of the 2017 GDP of the United States (in 2010 dollars), while the deaths are a bit higher than the population of North Korea.

Under Scenario 2, the annual economic costs are now almost two times the world's total GDP (in 2010 dollars) in 2017 and the annual number of deaths is a bit larger than the population of Thailand.

As we mentioned earlier, if the estimates for methane and CO_2 gas stored in permafrost regions are correct, and if we assume that all countries without enough water will desalinate (as opposed to their citizens migrating), then the temperatures in 2050 will reach 3.3° C above the average of the reference period under Scenario 1, and 25.9° C under Scenario 2. In effect, Scenario 2 renders the planet uninhabitable!

The annual economic costs therefore could reach $21.2 trillion under Scenario 1 and $353.3 trillion under Scenario 2. As for the annual deaths, they could reach 34.5 million under Scenario 1 and 161 million under Scenario 2.

Table 20: Summary of Annual Economic and Human Impacts by 2050

	Scenario 1		Scenario 2	
	Deaths/ extinctions	Economic loss $Trillions	Deaths/ extinctions	Economic loss $Trillions
Extinctions and deaths due to food shortages	99% of mammal species 47% of fish species 6.3% of plant species 39.3% of bird species 10,000,000 people	$4.000	All mammal species All fish species 50% of plant species All bird species 23,200,000 people	$9.300
Heatwaves - Direct - Com. diseases - Asthma	1,005,429 1,478,159 316,132	$0.8490 $0.0241 $0.3513	2,987,495 7,330,802 4,165,562	$3.5126 $0.1131 $5.2500
Droughts	Under extinctions	$0.0429	Under extinctions	$0.1953
Heavy rains, Floods & Landslides	8,697	$0.114	31,160	$0.519
Hurricanes	4,000	$0.103	4,886	$0.115
Sea level rise	No direct deaths	$8.000	No direct deaths	$22.200
Water Quantity		$1.800		$107.800
Water Quality	1,589,107	$0.0723	1,589,107	$0.1793
Air Quality - Direct - Indirect	11,288,871	$0.142 $0.304	30,345,222	$0.142 $3.449
TOTAL	25,690,395	$15.803	69,754,234	$152.775

Food

Between 1961 and 2016, and depending on the food type, food production increased between 2 and 4 times, as much as the population did (except for milk, see Table 21).

Some of the increased food production was the result of having more people living on this planet and some was due to people eating more than before (and wasting more[63]). How much of the increase in food production was due to the growth in people and how much was due to the growth in per capita consumption?

Table 21: Food Production Millions of Tonnes			
Food Type	1961	2016	% Rate of change 2016/1961
Crops	2,567.4	8,960.3	246%
Meat	71.3	329.9	362%
Fish	37.3	202.2	443%
Eggs	15.1	80.8	434%
Milk	344.2	798.5	132%
Source: FAOSTAT			

When it comes to crops, 43% of the increase in 2016 was due to the increase in consumption per person and 57% was due to the increase in the population. For meat, the increased per capita consumption accounted for 61% of the overall increase, for eggs 67%, for milk -7% and for fish 68%. So, for milk, all the increase was due to population growth since the average per capita consumption of milk decreased over time. Most of the increase in food from animal sources, then, was due to the increased prosperity in the world, rather than population growth, while for milk and crops it was the opposite.

Based on the relationship between food production, population, and general consumption[64], we arrive at the 2050 estimates shown in Table 22: Under Scenario 1, food production doubles, while under Scenario 2 it increases by eight-fold.

As we mentioned during our discussion of Malthus, agricultural land has been declining since 1998 due to the excessive use of water (salination) as well as climate change. We project that by 2050 we will lose another 4% of the agricultural land we had in 2015. In that case, the yield of crops per square kilometer of agricultural land must increase by 38% under Scenario 1, from

---

[63] Approximately, one third of the world's food produced for humans gets lost or wasted every year (about 1.3 billion tonnes), valued at US$990 billion – "Global Food Losses and Food Waste", FAO, 2011.

[64] These relationships are as follows:
Crops = 1,170,752,583 + 0.066445*Population + 0.0000965*GNE, with an R^2 = 99.4%
Meat = -58,641,706 + 0.02943*Population + 0.00000223*GNE, with an R^2 = 99.8%
Eggs = -23,176,011 + 0.077*Population + 0.00000059*GNE, with an R^2 = 99.1%
Milk = 333,106,680 - 0.0282*Population + 0.000009*GNE, with an R^2 = 98.7%
Fish = -56,087,125 + 0.02064*Population + 0.00000129*GNE, with an R^2 = 98.5%.

181 tonnes in 2015 to 251 tonnes in 2050, and by 484% under Scenario 2, from 181 tonnes in 2015 to 1,058 tonnes in 2050.

Food Type	2016	2050		% Rate of change 2050/2016	
		Scenario 1	Scenario 2	Scen. 1	Scen. 2
Crops	8,960.3	19,748.8	77,456.5	120%	764%
Meat	329.9	644.2	1,980.6	95%	500%
Fish	202.2	377.7	1,069.8	87%	429%
Eggs	80.8	162.3	517.0	101%	540%
Milk	798.5	1,682.3	6,501.5	111%	714%

Table 22: Food Production Millions of Tonnes

Source: FAOSTAT for 2016; my own estimates for 2050

Since in the previous 54 years (from 1961 to 2015) agricultural output per square kilometer increased only by 174%, it is hardly reasonable to expect that over the next 35 years it would increase by 484%, especially with water becoming scarcer, and with heavy downpours and droughts decimating plants and animals. So, the required food production for Scenario 2 is not achievable.

What about the 38% increase that is required under Scenario 1? Between 1961 and 2015, the crops and meat production increased annually by 2.2 tonnes per square kilometer. If this "technological" improvement continues to 2050, the world will only produce 12,447 million tonnes of crops and meat – far below the 20,392 million tonnes that are required for Scenario 1. And don't forget our earlier discussion on undernourished people that indicated that because of the rise in temperatures and the elimination of countless of species, food production is expected to decline by 11% – which means that we will only be able to produce 11,077 million tonnes of crops and meat leaving us with a food deficit of about 9,000 million tonnes (almost equal to the quantity of crops and meat we produced in 2016!).

Another way to look at the hopelessness of the situation is this: By 2050, there will be 40 countries, out of 212 with data, that will have farms of less than 0.72 acres per household - if you recall, this was the average size of the farms in Rwanda just prior to the genocide. These 40 counties will account for 618 million people.

Furthermore, it appears, after a cursory search of the web, that the minimum size of a farm necessary to feed a household of four is 2 acres. In 2050, there will be 85 countries that will have less than 2 acres of agricultural land per household! Most of these countries will have a household size greater than four people and a total population of 4.4 billion people (almost half of the world's population). This is a recipe for severe poverty, starvation, civil wars *à la* Rwanda style and mass migrations.

What about agricultural water? Under scenario 1, the water withdrawals for agriculture alone will increase to 73% of the total water withdrawals and reach 10.3 trillion cubic meters. Under Scenario 2 these withdrawals will reach 123.6 trillion cubic meters. Given that the world's total renewable water is only 54.7 trillion cubic meters, Scenario 2 is not feasible. But Scenario 1 will also be unfeasible for many countries, most of which are poor. Agriculture could use re-cycling, but there is so much recycling can do: every time the water is used its salinity increases, due to plant absorption. After a while, the water can no longer be used for irrigation.

< Conclusion >

"Heavy physical work, the care of home and children, petty quarrels with neighbors, films, football, beer, and above all, gambling filled up the horizon of their minds. To keep them in control was not difficult.... All that was required of them was a primitive patriotism which could be appealed to whenever it was necessary to make them accept longer working hours or shorter rations. And when they become discontented, as they sometimes did, their discontentment led nowhere, because being without general ideas, they could only focus it on petty specific grievances."
— George Orwell, 1984

Population, Economic Growth & Inequality

It is clear from the previous sections that creating a world where everyone is consuming the same amounts per capita is not possible at any level. The world simply does not have the required resources. But even if it did, the economic and human costs – not to mention the devastating impacts on other species - are such that will leave everyone worse off. And ironically, more so the people we were trying to help in the first place.

What about the first scenario where we keep advancing the way we always did? This is not feasible either because of its human and economic costs – a minimum of 26 million of annual deaths and $15.8 trillion in annual damages is well beyond "feasible" (these impacts could easily reach $21.2 trillion in damages and 34.5 million in deaths) – not to count the billions of sufferers from acute or chronic diseases, the increased local conflicts, and the mass migrations. If we were terrified by the 60 million people who died during the six years of WWII, then we should be triply terrified by the 156 million people who will die under Scenario 1 over the same time period – and keep dying in 6-year cycles.

In this case then, isn't better to give up the idea of reaching that goal and avoid all the misery that will be inflicted upon the existing, and future, populations? Think of two castaways on an isolated Pacific island that has a single tree. Imagine further that the tree produces enough fruits to provide our castaways with famine level calories. Then it is neither smart nor fair to bring into the world a third person (a baby) that will require a third of the food – because at least one of them will die (the number will depend on whether they die in sequence or simultaneously). Neither is it smart to try to increase food production by methods that are known to kill trees – because then everyone dies. Thus, it will be better not to have the baby in the first place since having it produces an outcome that is worse than what it was prior to having the baby.

Most of the world's attention these days is focused on trying to find technological solutions to environmental problems; solutions that will allow us to keep multiplying and consuming at will. In other words, even if some of these solutions are successful, they are nevertheless temporary patches that treat the symptoms, not the causes of the problem. No-one in their right mind would believe that if the population was going to reach 50 billion people in 2050, instead of 9.8 billion, everything would be peachy. Developing fusion power may solve most of the energy problems, but we will still need to feed, clothe, entertain, transport and shelter these people. And the sector entitled "Agriculture, Forestry and Other Land Uses" is the second largest source of greenhouse gas emissions (24%), not far behind the energy sector (25%).

Some government programs recognize the problem and attempt to curb consumption. For example, carbon pricing attempts to deal with climate change by reducing the demand for energy and by providing incentives to the companies that produce energy to find technological solutions that will reduce their greenhouse gas emissions. Unfortunately, partly because there are no short-term substitutes available, the demand for energy is inelastic[65], i.e., it does not respond much to a price increase, especially in the short-run (a 10% increase in the price of energy could reduce demand in the short-run by as little as 0.9% and by as much as 7.6%). As such, the demand will not be reduced by much and hence the profits of the energy producers will not be affected by much thus removing any incentives to innovate. Furthermore, since energy producers are not in the business of producing technological solutions to problems related to climate change, it is doubtful that they would be capable of doing so even if the incentives worked. Under these conditions, then, carbon pricing becomes just another income-grabbing scheme by governments – a scheme that has regressive impacts, i.e., it taxes poor people, in relative terms, more than rich.

Some people think that having children does not impose externalities on anyone else and as such this should be a private decision. But as we saw in the previous pages, population growth does impose severe externalities on

---

[65] "A meta-analysis on the price elasticity of energy demand", Xavier Labandeira, José M. Labeaga and Xiral López-Otero, EUI Working Papers, 2016; in this paper the authors indicate that short-run elasticities range in the literature from -0.09 to -0.76.

the existing, and the future, population through its impact on the environment.

So, what is there to do? Well, for one thing, there should be more aggressive efforts to stem population growth worldwide – maybe a target of one or two babies per family would be a good start. More money should be going into family planning, especially in the countries with high population growth, and some incentives could also work in stemming the tide – for example, free contraceptives and financial incentives not to have more than one child could help and so could the disappearance of the pro-life folks (although their actions are not motived by a need to increase population).

There is an argument that education and industrialization will help solve the problem of population growth because as soon as people become educated, they move to an urban center, get a job, and stop having as many children as before. This is really a naïve view.

For one thing, although it is true that this phenomenon has occurred in many Western countries, it simply took too long for this process to work. As we saw earlier, our time-frame is only 32 years with all sorts of nasty things happening within that period. The UN population projections to 2100 (i.e., 82 years in the future) still show a positive growth all the way through to 2100. Europe's population growth declined to zero percent for the first time in 1997 – that is 46 years after our starting point, 1950.

The proportion of China's population (15+) with a tertiary degree was 2.17% in 2010 as opposed to 27.8% for the United States. The Chinese economic zones program, which started in 1979, has managed to raise per capita GDP to US$17,000, as opposed to US$59,500 for the United States, but only after 39 years. And in the process, China has become the biggest emitter of greenhouse gasses (12.5 million kilo-tonnes, as opposed to 6.3 million kilo-tonnes for the US). And India, which is the third largest polluter at 3 million kilo-tonnes, has a GDP per capita of only US$7,200. To wait for these countries to educate their population and hope that social forces will work their magic and reduce their family size is rather unrealistic. And let us not forget that greenhouse gasses persist in the atmosphere for centuries and as such, it is just not helpful to reduce population growth 50 years from now.

Second, even if the education solution could work faster, the decrease in population, and hence consumption, will have to exceed the increase in per capita consumption that will follow when people become more educated and more middle-class[66]. And as we saw earlier, most of the environmental problems are not caused by population growth per se, but rather by increased per capita spending. And this, i.e., telling educated, higher-income people not to consume more than before, may be a much more difficult sell than convincing them to have smaller families.

Third, some countries that have very large families today (triple in size to those in Europe) have already industrialized - in the sense that they now have some of the highest per capita GDP in the world, higher than that of the US – and yet they are still having large families (e.g., the oil-producing Arab countries). Presumably cultural habits play a role here.

Finally, population growth, no matter how small, drives our obsession with economic growth by necessity. For example, if a country's GDP is $1 million and this country has 10 people, then the per capita GDP will be $100,000. But if the GDP stays the same and the population increases to 20 people, then the per capita GDP will be $50,000. So, to maintain our standards of living, the economy needs to grow if the population is growing. But if the population is not growing, we do not necessarily need to grow the economy, especially if we are content with what we already have.

The world, then, seems to be in a catch-22 situation. If income gets re-distributed, the recipients will increase consumption which will then aggravate the environmental impacts. If income does not get re-distributed, poor countries will continue to have children, since they cannot even afford birth control, thus contributing to global problems through migration, environmental impacts, and local conflicts (conflicts that could potentially become global conflicts).

So, under what circumstances could equality work? Well, from the numbers we have seen thus far, we could safely declare that we have already passed the tipping point as far as environmental impacts are concerned. But, for argument's sake, let us say that the 2016 level of GNE ($77 trillion) is sustainable in the long run, from an environmental impact point of view. If we use again the US as our reference country ($54,527 of per capita GNE in 2016 in 2010 US dollars) then we will need to boost the per capita GNE of all the countries lower than the US (206 of them) by an average of $40,436. But at

---

[66] The Average Propensity to Consume, which tell us how much consumption increases on average due to an increase in disposable income was found to be 0.80 in Bangladesh, 0.74 in India, 0.91 in Nepal, 0.81 in Pakistan and 0.95 in Sri Lanka, between 1985 and 2013. This means that a 10% increase in income in, say, Bangladesh will increase consumption by 8%. See "Estimation of Consumption Functions: The Case of Bangladesh, India, Nepal, Pakistan And Sri Lanka", Khalid Khan, Sabeen Anwar, Manzoor Ahmed & M. Abdul Kamal, Pakistan Business Review, April 2015.

the same time, we will need to keep global GNE at $77 trillion. This can only be achieved if the world's population is 1.4 billion. In other words, equality is feasible if the world's population declined from 7.5 billion in 2016 to 1.4 billion – an 81% reduction! If people stopped having babies tomorrow, it will take us about 64 years to reach that level of population through attrition. But then, halleluiah!

This then brings us back to the question that Malthus was asking, with a slight modification to include equality: "Is there an optimum population size where people could enjoy the fruits of their labours in near equality?". The answer is yes, provided that the $77 trillion of GNE is environmentally sustainable (which is not). And that size is 1.4 billion people (about the size of the world's population in 1850).

Alternatively, if reducing the number of people on this planet is politically a non-starter, then we can ask the same question but now substitute the word "consumption" for the word "population". That is, what is the optimal level of per capita consumption (GNE) if the population grows to 9.8 billion in 2050? Assuming again that the 2016 level of GNE ($77 trillion) is environmentally sustainable then this implies that per capita consumption will have to be $7,867. That's 24% lower than the per capita consumption we had in 2016 ($10,296), and 56% lower than the per capita GNE we are expected to have in 2050 ($19,016) – which we will most likely never achieve due to the excessive costs of climate change and other pollutants.

So, the choices are rather gloomy. We either reduce the population level, and with it the overall level of consumption, but we keep the per capita consumption high, or we keep the population level high, and reduce per capita consumption by a quarter over the 2016 levels. Either way, population, or consumption, or both will have to be reduced either by choice (and hence minimize the unpleasantness of reaching our desired outcome), or by the consequences of our inactivity (in this case the planet will make that choice for us and lead us to the same outcome but after a lot of pain).

Political Organization

What also becomes clear here is that the present system of world governance is not very helpful. When resources get scarce, people get frightened and countries become insular. Nationalism flourishes and people think that by closing their borders, or by attacking someone else – within or without – would solve their problems. But these solutions did not work in the past. As a matter of fact, nationalism has left us with a terrible legacy of inhumanity and destruction.

If a country decides to reduce its economic growth, or its population, or to charge the full costs of greenhouse gas emissions to its producers and consumers, then there are no guarantees that others will do the same. The Payoff Matrix below shows the options that countries are facing when it comes to greenhouse gasses.

	Payoff Matrix	
	I reduce greenhouse gasses	**I do not reduce greenhouse gasses**
Everyone else reduces greenhouse gasses	We avoid catastrophe, but my relative position stays the same	We avoid catastrophe and my relative position improves
No-one else reduces greenhouse gasses	We do not avoid catastrophe and my relative position deteriorates	We do not avoid catastrophe and my relative position stays the same

If country A chooses to reduce, say, its greenhouse gas emissions, then the best outcome for A will be when everyone else does the same, while the worst outcome will be when no-one else reduces their greenhouse gas emissions.

If country A chooses not to reduce its greenhouse gas emissions then the best outcome will be when everyone else does, while the worst outcome will be when no-one else does.

So, what is the rational choice here? Since the benefits of the "I don't reduce" strategy are greater than those of the "I reduce" strategy (avoid catastrophe and country A's relative position improves) and its costs are lower (country A's relative position does not get worse), then country A will choose not to reduce its greenhouse gas emissions. But, so will everyone else and the outcome will be that the catastrophe is not avoided. This is a classic prisoner's dilemma scenario that is played out by our current political organizations.

It is not, however, only countries that use this kind of calculus. Individuals use it too. No-one thinks, and correctly, that by them having an extra baby or a second TV will cause the world to end. So, they have the baby and the second TV, hoping that others will not do the same. But this is how everyone thinks and as such there are too many babies and too many TVs.

As an example of the consequences of the free-rider problem, consider the recent riots in France (the yellow jackets) despite the fact that public opinion polls[67] suggest that 86% of French people "support their own country limiting greenhouse gas emissions as part of an international agreement" and 83% say that "people will have to make major changes in the way they live". So, why the 2018 riots in response to a tax on gasoline consumption?

Well, because: a) the United States, the second largest emitter of greenhouse gasses, gave notice in August of 2017 that it will withdraw from the Paris agreement, b) China's gas emissions in the first three months of 2018 increased by 4% over the same period in 2017 and the country, which is the largest greenhouse gas emitter in the world, is now headed for its largest annual increase in greenhouse gasses since 2011[68], and c) in 2017 the average gasoline price in France was $5.87 per gallon, as opposed to $3.26 for the world average, $3.56 for China and $2.69 for the US[69]. All of these facts, then, imply that the major emitters of greenhouse gasses are not in compliance with the Paris agreement – a non-compliance that should make French people feel like suckers in doing their part (France accounts for only 1% of the global greenhouse gas emissions as opposed to 26% for China, 15% for the United States and 6.4% for India).

Thus, we need a political structure that can enforce what is agreed upon collectively and, at the same time, is able to assist those impacted. In other words, we need a global government with fiscal and monetary control of the world's affairs (i.e., neither a UN nor an EU type of world government).

Designed to Fail

Now a world government is a bit of a lofty dream that has an almost zero probability of being implemented in the near or the far future. And the worse things get, the smaller the probability that it will happen as more and more countries embrace nationalism. But we could do something about the designed obsolescence built into every consumer product.

When companies purposely build things that are designed to break down and be disposed off within 5 years, the waste of resources is tremendous[70]. The strategy is good for the companies engaged in it, but it is not good for

---

[67] "Public opinion on the climate challenge: a trip around the world before COP21", Pew Research Center, November 6, 2015.
[68] "Dramatic surge in China carbon emissions signals climate danger", May 2018, Unearthed.
[69] "France's gas prices among highest in the world", Axios, December, 2018.
[70] "Industry" is the third largest producer of greenhouse gas emissions (21%). Its emissions come from the burning of fossil fuels for energy on site as well as from chemical, metallurgical and mineral transformation processes and waste management activities.

the society because there is nothing that we produce today that captures in its price the full social costs of its production and consumption.

But why is it that the market system has not come up with an answer? Why is it that some company does not come along and design products that will last and hence drive the others out of the market? Is it because there is collusion? That will not be much of a stretch to believe since most markets are organized as oligopolies. Furthermore, the free market system is terrible at internalizing externalities. In both of these cases, then, governments need to intervene at the global level.

Let's Look at the Nuclear Power Option Again

An option that could help reduce the greenhouse gas emissions involves the replacement of fossil fuels[71] with nuclear power. Unfortunately, nuclear power has had a bad history, more perceptual than real[72], starting with the US choosing to fund the water-cooling nuclear plants back in the early 50s rather than the salt-cooled reactors.

Conventional nuclear plants today take too long to build and cost too much. After six years of building two conventional reactors in South Carolina, the power company in charge of the project gave up after sinking $9 billion into it. Another reactor in Finland is already six years behind schedule and $6.5 billion over budget, and another one in France is nine years behind schedule. Given their high construction costs and the extensive approvals processes these plants have to go through, electricity produced by nuclear plants is presently not competitive with fossil fuels, especially natural gas.

But there are the 4th generation nuclear reactors that are much smaller, easier to build and safer – some of them, like the one promoted by Bill Gates, even burn the radioactive waste! At the present time, these reactors are at least 10-20 years out in terms of commercialization, partly because their development has been left to private investors and partly because of the excessive regulations.

---

[71] The burning of oil, coal and natural gas for electricity and heat production is the largest source of greenhouse gas emissions (25%). When the entire fuel life cycle is taken into account, which includes the mining and manufacturing of the engines and fuel needed, nuclear plants emit 100 times less carbon per megawatt-hour than coal plants and 50 times less than natural gas plants; they even emit less than solar plants!

[72] According to Gallup Poll, the US public opinion on nuclear energy has gone from a high of 62% in favour in 2010 to a low of 44% in favour in 2016.

But if utilities were treated as public goods, then the benefits of building them could easily exceed their costs since the benefits will now include the social benefits from reduced greenhouse gas emissions (benefits that are presently not captured by the private sector). Government grants, equal perhaps to the social benefits, along with some modernization of the approvals process, could then speed up commercialization.

Finally, there is the future option of fusion plants that promise unlimited clean power without radioactive waste. But these plants are nowhere near commercialization – they are not even near producing more electrical output than the electrical input they require! But the US managed to split the atom in just four years (the Manhattan Project) when the need arose. Why can't we repeat the Manhattan Project but now for fusion?

Let's Also Treat Transportation as a Public Good

Transportation (cars, trains, boats, and planes) is the fourth largest source of greenhouse gas emissions globally (14%). As was the case with power plants, leaving the management of the transportation sector to private industry results in sub-optimal levels of investment from a social point of view.

Private companies making decisions on how much to spend on R&D for engines powered by non-fossil fuels, or building trains and train-tracks that are powered by electricity (as long as the electricity does not come from plants powered by fossil fuels), or developing networks of stations for charging electric cars, will only invest to the point where it is profitable for them, i.e., they will never take into account the social benefits of lowering the greenhouse gas emissions.

This then provides another argument either for government grants in those areas or for taking over their development and creating a new Manhattan Project for engines that do not depend on fossil fuels.

But We Also Need to Be Fair to Developing Countries…

If we had a world government, fairness would not be much of a problem as the government would allocate resources according to the needs of its citizens – at least in theory. But we do not, and so for the Western countries to say to a developing country "don't cut down your rainforest" or "cut down pollution" is not fair because the Western countries have already done exactly that in order to develop – unless of course a majority was in favour of the principle "first-come-first-served", which does not seem likely given people's general preference for fair rules.

If the West wants developing countries to reduce their pollution levels, or save their rainforests, or reduce their populations, they could just pay them to do so. In that way, some transfer of resources from rich countries to poor countries would occur, improving the existing unequal distribution of income, while at the same time avoiding environmental impacts. Building (for free) a nuclear plant or a sun-powered plant in a country that is poor and dependent exclusively on coal to produce its electricity, is not just good for that the poor country; it is also good for the rich country that is financing it since pollution and climate change do not respect national boundaries.

But all of these actions would require some coordinated effort among the countries of the West and some agreement on how to share the transfer payments. And since the free rider problem could raise its ugly head again, this is another argument in support for a world government.

...And Respect Democratic Principles

The political establishments of the West need to improve in at least two areas: First, they need to stop treating their own citizens like morons who have nothing to say about anything. The citizens of a country are not there to just help a few others develop a career and get rich. They are there to express their opinions and preferences about issues, not just elect people they scarcely know. The current political system has been around for 73 years now, since the end of WWII, and it has very little to show that is generally good and a lot that is generally bad.

Second, the West needs to stop living this schizophrenic existence when it comes to democracy. The US is the prime example of the existing double standard. Americans seem to believe in democracy and are jealously protective of it in their own country. But when it comes to other countries, all these principles go out the window.

Recently, the Americans have been all in knots about Russia interfering in their 2016 presidential elections. But since the end of WWII, the US has done just that to countries in Central and South America, the Caribbean, the Middle East, Southeast Asia and even in Greece – and much worse, if assassinations are worse than fake news stories on Facebook. How fair or democratic is it to sabotage democratically elected governments because of a pathological fear of socialism or a pathological need to protect "American interests" – meaning promoting an American company's right to exploit another country's resources or to access its markets?

As things stand, the West can be characterized as driven by three principles in the following order: a) the unfettered pursuit of economic growth, b) the excessive pursuit of consumerism (in order to help the first principle; so this principle is not a stand-alone principle, but rather a means of achieving the first), and c) humanism, as long as humanism does not interfere with the first two principles (observe the affectionate cozying up to, and the accommodation of, rich dictators – from the communist types in China to the traditional ones in the Middle East – in order to get their business).

Although, in general, there may be nothing wrong with the West's principles, if supported by a majority – to find something wrong with them would require a comparison to the "right" principles, which are elusive in the absence of majority support – these principles may be wrong for organizing life in other countries, especially if these other countries do not exactly espouse them (for example, aboriginal communities do not espouse the West's business approach to life). However, the West is hell-bent on turning everyone into themselves – whether this is done by the lure of consumer goods, or by making their assistance conditional on the recipient accepting the West's way of life, or by simply bribing or threatening the recipient's government. Any assistance that the West wishes to offer to developing countries should in principle be unconditional – as long as a dictator does not run the developing country – and it should be the local people who decide how or whether to use the assistance.

How does this relate to our discussion of climate change, population growth, and democracy? Well, it does because a) it reveals a scant adherence to democratic principles, b) it infuses the world with principles that are responsible for the excessive environmental impacts we observe today and c) it leaves the developing countries in a never-ending cycle of chasing after the West's consumerism – never-ending because one's satisfaction with the 2017 iPhone evaporates as soon as the 2018 model is out.

< Appendix A >

Alma: "Are you depressed by what you just read?"
John: "Yes"
Alma: "Well, read on, maybe this will lighten up your mood!"
John: "I hope so because I am ready to commit some act of unspecified violence."
– The Depressing Dialogues, Unpublished, Anonymous, 2019

Fairness vs. Equality

Although discourse on economic inequality is not new, recently it feels like a daily occurrence in newspapers, broadcasts, and magazines. A Google search of English language publications gives the following results for these keywords: "Top 1%": 233 million; "Income inequality": 66 million; "Income distribution": 166 million.

These results seem to indicate that we are sufficiently concerned with this topic not only to take it to the streets (*à la* Occupy) but also to talk about it endlessly. Which is good, in the sense that democracy cannot function properly without discourse. But it could also be bad if, after a majority reaches a decision, these protestations persist simply because a minority desires a different outcome.

Has a majority reached a decision on this issue? Well, there is no country in the world where people have expressed their preferences directly on this subject. Hence the discourse and the demonstrations will continue in representative democracies until it becomes the sole issue on a party's pre-election platform and hence, if such a party ever gets elected, reveals the majority's preference. But until such time, can we get a glimpse of what the general attitude is towards equality?

The evidence appears to be somewhat contradictory. On the one hand, numerous laboratory-studies (i.e., dragging a few people, mainly students, in a room to participate in experiments designed by academics) have found that people have a natural aversion to inequality. On the other hand, when polling studies ask about real-world distributions of wealth, people exhibit a preference for certain degree of inequality – and this latter result seems to hold across demographics, across the political spectrum, and across countries.

A recent review article[73] on the subject argues that: a) many of the laboratory studies confound fairness with equality because they are designed in a way that equal outcomes are also fair outcomes – hence the apparent contradiction with population studies; b) people seem to be bothered not by economic inequality per se, but rather by economic unfairness; and c) when there is a clash between fairness and equality, people seem to prefer a fair inequality to an unfair equality.

Naturally, people's preference for inequality is constrained by the price they would have to pay and their ability to pay it. What is the price of inequality? Well, apart from the moral indignation that we feel, the 20th Century has had 310 major revolts (3.1 revolts per year excluding wars between nations), while the 21st Century has had 98 and counting[74] (that is 5.8 revolts per year; an increase of 86% over the previous century).

There are the obvious direct economic and human costs associated with these revolts, but there may also be some indirect ones associated with changes in political regimes. When such changes occur, there are repercussions for those who prefer the status quo. But if the supporters of the status quo were a minority, then that is not a problem for a democratic society at large. But if they were a majority, then that is a serious problem for the society at large. More often than not, successful rebels do not constitute a majority at the society level, and neither do the people who eventually form the government constitute a majority within the rebel groups. For example, the Bolsheviks were neither a majority group within Russia nor a majority group among the communists when they took over the 1917 revolution in Russia.

Alright, inequality has psychological, economic, and human costs associated with it and people are more concerned about fairness than they are about equality, but what do we mean by fairness[75]?

☞ ⑨ ⁊⋞ ②

Traditionally, it has been philosophers, political scientists, and economists who study the concept of justice, and its twin sister fairness. In the 20th Century there are three prominent theories:

---

[73] "Why people prefer unequal societies", *Nature Human Behaviour,* 2017, C. Starmans, M. Sheskin, & P. Bloom.
[74] Wikipedia; the counts include revolts up to the end of 2017
[75] For more on fairness see my book "On Democracy: A Novel", Amazon, 2012

Foley[76] argues that an allocation of resources is equitable if no one envies anyone else's bundle and it is fair[77] if no one can become better off by moving to a new allocation without hurting someone else.

This definition brings efficiency into the concept of fairness, in the sense that if an allocation is not efficient then everyone could become better off by moving to an efficient one without even invoking any concepts of fairness. It also brings into the definition of fairness the concept of envy which is problematic as it introduces strategic behaviour: if I really dislike someone and I know that this person likes his own allocation better than mine, I could declare that I desire his allocation more than mine just to spite him – a declaration that will trigger a cascade of exchanges until a new efficient allocation is reached where no-one desires the bundle of anyone else.

On the one hand, this is a brilliant definition of equity because it allows individuals to judge an allocation based on their own preferences and not based on some arithmetic distribution of resources. For example, suppose we had two individuals, four apples and four oranges. And assume that one individual prefers apples to oranges while the other prefers the opposite. Then giving to each of them two apples and two oranges will be neither equitable nor fair since the individual who preferred the apples would want to trade his oranges for apples and so will the individual who preferred oranges to apples.

On the other hand, however, this is not a very practical definition: First, there is the problem of having a limited supply of universally desired bundles – clearly, everyone would want to get Bill Gate's bundle, but there is only one of it. And to arrive at an outcome where no-one desires anyone else's bundle would require an infinite sequence of musical chairs without any roadmap of how to do it.

Second, there is the problem of defining what the "bundle" contains. Does it contain only commodities or does it also include the effort a person has put into acquiring the bundle, any elements of chance involved in obtaining it, and this person's natural and acquired skills (i.e., a person's biological inheritance and social environment)? And if so, how would we divvy up these attributes to get to an equitable bundle? Even more importantly, how do we decide in a fair way what the bundle should include and how do we go about (in a fair way) achieving an equitable and fair allocation? This, unfortunately,

---

[76] Foley, D., 1967, Resource allocation and the public sector. *Yale Economic Essays*, 7, 45—98.
[77] This condition was added later by Schmeidler, D., and Yaari, M., "Fair Allocations," unpublished, 1971.

brings us back to the definition of fairness and reveals that Foley's work does not address the issue of how to get to a fair allocation in a fair way.

Rawls[78], investigates what principles should one adopt in evaluating the fairness of a state of the world. These principles, according to Rawls, are the ones that an individual would adopt if he were in an "original" position of total ignorance about himself and about where he might end up in the society (i.e., whether he is going to be poor, middle-class or rich).

Assuming that individuals are infinitely risk-averse (I guess risk aversion has not been wiped out by the veil of ignorance!), an assumption not explicitly made by Rawls but needed to obtain his results, then individuals would choose, according to him, basic liberties (freedom of speech, the right to vote, the right to hold property, etc.) and the principle that prohibits inequality in wealth unless this inequality works for the benefit of the worst-off individual in the society.

Rawls' thought experiment is rather nonsensical: it is impossible for anyone to decide what principles of justice to adopt in the absence of any information about themselves and about the consequences of their choices. For example, choosing principles that result in a distribution of wealth that is independent of people's abilities and effort, may lead to a reduction in effort and innovation by those who see their contributions as more significant than those of their "equals". This, in turn, could have detrimental impacts on everyone, including the worst-off individuals. In this sense, this scheme will result in an inefficient allocation and hence not fair according to Foley.

Furthermore, why is it fair to derive the principles of justice behind a veil of ignorance and not behind a veil of full information about one's own preferences and position in society? Clearly, the derived principles, in this case, will be vastly different than Rawls'. But - one might object - this full information scheme cannot lead to principles of justice because people will be suggesting principles based on selfish motives: if I know that my position in society is going to be a privileged one, then I would suggest principles that protect this position (e.g., property rights, the right to inheritance, etc.). And if I know that I will be poor, I will be suggesting principles that take me out of my poverty (e.g., no right to hold property and no right to inheritance). But that is exactly what the risk-averse individuals in Rawls' thought experiment are also doing – that is, they are looking after their own self-interests. They suggest Rawls' principles precisely because, in the absence of information, they want to protect themselves from unpleasant outcomes. In any event, like Foley's concept of fairness, Rawls' ideas do not address the way to achieve a

---

[78] Rawls, J., A Theory of Justice, Harvard University Press, 1971

fair allocation (in a fair way) in a society that is already experiencing a given distribution of wealth.

Nozick[79] suggests that the principles of justice cannot be based on end-states but instead these principles should be based on the procedures that generate these end-states. If the process is just, then whatever outcome occurs is also just. And what is a just process for Nozick? Justice in *acquisition* – the appropriation of resources no one has owned before – justice in *transfer* – the governing of how one can own something owned by someone else – and justice in *rectification* – the governing of the process of settling disputes about *acquisition* and *transfer*. But what are just *acquisition, transfer,* and *rectification*? Nozick's theory at this point becomes either arbitrary (e.g., his insistence that individual rights should trump every other consideration or subject matter) or circular (i.e., a just acquisition is an acquisition that is just!). Furthermore, why is it fair to deny people the right to define the rules or the outcome or both? Isn't this denial a contradiction of Nozick's unconditional acceptance of individual rights?

Of the three theories described above, Nozick's is the only one dealing with a fair procedure, while the other two deal with fair allocations, or end-states. How likely are any of these three theories to win a majority? Since at any given time some people have a vested interest in the status quo, while others may have different ideas (there is an inexhaustible list of factors that could enter the scene and cause disagreements), they are unlikely to get a majority. These theories form opinions on how the world should be, given some assumptions about human behaviour and the author's personal beliefs, rather than how people desire their world to be – a desire that materializes in a direct democracy through the exercise of one's voting rights. As such, if there are any general principles of justice in a democratic society, then it is the right to vote and the principle that all is decided by vote.

From the literature (see Starmans et all), it appears that people have a favorable bias towards fair procedures rather than equal outcomes, a fact that seems to validate Nozick's theory more than the other two, or at least Nozick's primary thesis that it is the rules we need to address and not the outcome.

But why can we not address both, the rules and the outcomes? Because defining fair outcomes independently of fair rules cannot guarantee that the rule will lead to the desired outcome. The fairness of an outcome can only be evaluated by referring to the circumstances that led to it. To ask whether an outcome is fair without referring to the process and circumstances that led to

---

[79] Nozick, R., Anarchy State and Utopia, Basic Books, 1974.

it has no meaning. For example, one could not evaluate the fairness of the statement "Individual A is a millionaire and individual B is not" without knowing something about how individuals A and B came to be what they are and without having accepted some rules about what constitutes a fair remuneration. As such, an outcome is fair only if the rules that produced it were fair. Declaring an outcome as fair without knowing which fair rule could generate it, and at the same time defining independently a rule as fair, would produce incompatible and unexpected results.

On the other hand, this is not true for economic equality. That is, one could easily determine whether a distribution of income is equal or not, without a reference to anything else. In the above example, we can easily declare that this outcome is not an equal outcome since individual A has more money than B. As such, equal outcomes would rarely be fair since the unique rules that generate them may not be accepted as fair rules.

Do fair procedures produce equal outcomes? Not in general. Economic outcomes depend on people's widely varied skills, intelligence, luck, inheritance, effort, upbringing, education, preferences, etc. As such, the only rule that will produce equal economic outcomes is the rule that eliminates inheritance, compensates everyone the same irrespective of what and how much each one produces, and does not permit any savings (to permit savings based on individual inter-temporal preferences, and hence investment, would cause income to be unequally distributed after some time). But such a dictatorial system will result in a very inefficient outcome. Which means that everyone could become better off (i.e., increase the wealth of everyone) by allowing some people to have more than others. Such an outcome then could not possibly be considered fair since it penalizes everyone in the society for the sake of a concept (apart from the fact that this rule is unlikely to be accepted by a majority).

What about the free market system? Well, the free market system will never produce an outcome where wealth is equal across all people because of all the different factors we just mentioned that determine one's economic position in life. Furthermore, even if we were able, through intervention, to achieve economic equality, this outcome would not be sustainable in the long-run. As long as the free market is in operation, it will eventually cause income to be unequally distributed again and thus require continuous interventions to maintain it – interventions which are not part of the free market system, and hence not necessarily fair, especially if we had accepted the free market system as fair.

Could unfair procedures achieve fair outcomes? Sure. Any system that espouses Machiavelli's principles that the end justifies the means will do just that. But in this case the fairness of the outcome will have to be defined independently of the fairness of the procedure. And as we mentioned, it is not possible to define an outcome as fair independently of the procedure that achieved it. For example, if we define as fair the outcome where "people without hair have double the income of people with hair", then we cannot turn around and independently find a fair rule that would hopefully lead us to that outcome. The only rule that can get us there is the dictatorial rule where we take away the income of everyone and redistribute it according to the requirements of our outcome. Any other procedure will produce outcomes that clash with our desired one. And, as we mentioned, people seem to have a favorable bias towards fair procedures. This discussion, then, lead us to accept Nozick's statement that as long as the rule is fair, whatever the outcome, it is also fair.

When people across the political spectrum, across demography and across countries have an aversion to unfair procedures, why do we observe such bitter fights about political systems, elections, trade frameworks, compensation levels for CEOs, the promotion of colleagues, and the like (even in Nozick's minimal state, which includes only police, the military and judicial services, there will be disagreements about how to share its costs in a fair way or how minimal the state should be)?

The processes that we are exploring here are rules that are set up to answer questions of a collective nature ("private" questions such as "Is it fair that John likes ice cream?" have no meaning). For example, if the question is "how do we financially compensate a team's members?", then a possible rule could be: "compensation should be commensurate to the contributions of each team member to the team's output". But is this a fair rule?

Here we will take the position that a process is fair: a) if we have agreed in advance of its application that it is fair (or in a democracy, if a majority has agreed that it is fair), and b) if we also agree afterward that its application adhered to the rules we originally agreed upon. In other words, fairness in a democracy is what the majority decides it to be at any given place, time and circumstances.

Our disagreements, then, arise because of two reasons: First, there is no general agreement of what constitutes a fair rule because there are simply too many factors that could be proposed as conditions for a rule's fairness: Should initial endowments, not only economic but also biological ones, be part of the rule? The compensation rule mentioned earlier accepts biological inheritance and upbringing as being fair, but labour unions would always object to such a compensation scheme. Should individual rights, including property rights, be paramount? And if yes, which ones? Should someone's place of birth, family upbringing, gender or education be part of the rule as well? Should chance-outcomes be part of the rule? Should the rule be based on individual preferences or on "divine commands" inscribed in some "holy" book?

Second, we also disagree because in the ex-post monitoring of the rule's application some of us believe that the rule did not follow what we thought we had agreed upon – either because people cheated or because governments (not necessarily supported by a majority) had modified these procedures by imposing their own rules.

For example, if we agree that the free market system is a fair rule, then we would be hard pressed to find a pure free market system in existence. Instead what we find are heavily regulated market systems. And the powerful among us usually influence the choice of regulations in order to gain an economic advantage. This issue is especially troubling in representative democracies because there is significantly more room there for the powerful to influence the people's representatives.

Where is the proof of that? Well, according to free-market theories, labour should be compensated according to its marginal product. In other words, compensation should be tied to labour productivity. In a recent study from the Pew Research Centre[80], the real (in 2018 dollars) average hourly wage in the US grew between 1964 and 2018 (that's 54 years) by a pathetic 12%, from $20.27 to $22.65. At the same time, labour productivity grew by 169%[81]! If the "free market" had worked properly, the hourly average wage should have been closer to $55 – that is more than double than what it is in the real world!

And where have the gains of labour's productivity gone? Naturally, to the high-income earners and to corporate profits – real, in 2002 prices, corporate profits after tax[82] increased by 419% over the same period[83], while the median household income of the top 5% earners increased by 112% between 1967 and 2016[84]! And yet, many Americans believe that their economic system is a fair one! Is this belief based on facts, or on propaganda by those who benefit from the status quo? Well, clearly it is not based on facts, hence....

─────────

[80] "For most U.S. workers, real wages have barely budged in decades", D. Desilver, Pew Research Centre, 2018.
[81] US Bureau of Labor Statistics.
[82] With adjustments made for inventories and capital consumption.
[83] US Bureau of Economic Analysis.
[84] US Census Bureau, "Income and Poverty in the United States", 2016.

We have taken the position here that fair rules are processes for answering specific collective questions, rather than a universal rule that answers any question under any circumstances. We have also stated without proof that because there are too many factors that could enter a fair rule as conditions, it is unlikely to get agreement on what constitutes a fair rule. Here we will formalize the non-existence of such an agreement over fair rules.

Recognizing then that: a) in human societies it is the people living in those societies that define "what is", and b) different people will have different ideas about fairness, the question becomes: "can we find a rule that will aggregate people's preferences on the subject and render a socially preferred fair procedure"? An example of such an aggregating rule will be the one used by the military to decide on tactics, strategy, and any other military matters: "no matter what the soldiers think, the army does what the General decides".

In what follows, we are not going to consider "divine commands" as requiring special treatment, notwithstanding the fact that billions of people around the world *appear* to accept "divine commands" over individual preferences.

The reason is fourfold: First, the search here is for a rule that aggregates individual preferences and expresses the Will of the people. "Divine rules", on the other hand, express, in theory, the Will of "God". But which God? If people do not accept these divine rules, then these rules do not fit in our present discussion. Presumably, no-one would consider the "divine commands" of a religion that has zero followers, or a religion that does not exist! If, on the other hand, people accepted these "divine commands", then, by definition, these "commands" are now part of the individual preferences. Hence, their presence or absence from the final selection of an aggregating rule does not negate our approach.

Second, "divine commands" are usually not aggregating rules, but rather behavioural rules. Aggregating rules do not tell people what to do, but rather how to arrive at a social decision. For example, the simple majority rule says that the social outcome is the one preferred by 50% of the voters plus one. Or the army rule, we mentioned earlier, says that the General decides on tactics, but it does not tell the General what the tactic is. On the other hand, religious rules are all about telling people what to do, e.g., "don't eat pork", "love thy neighbour", "atone for your sins", etc. This then defeats the purpose of trying to find a rule that aggregates individual preferences since religious commands completely ignore these preferences – you must avoid eating pork whether you like it or not.

Third, since a very small number of humans wrote all "divine commands" a long time ago, we are accepting their preferences as the only ones that count for all eternity! Which also defeats the purpose of seeking the Will of the people today.

Finally, there are volumes of other rules, created over the years by those in religious authority (who are clearly human), that accompany "holy books" as interpretations, clarifications, or reconciliations. And more often, it is these latter rules that are being practiced by the followers of a religion. This implies that the original rules were neither clear nor logically consistent. As such, why should a society adopt rules that may be illogical, unclear, and may not express the Will of God, but rather that of a clergy?

But, let us get back to our aggregating rule for individual preferences. Is there one? Alas! There is no such an aggregating rule[85] if there are more than two fair procedures under consideration and if we also require that this aggregating rule possesses some basic logical properties to avoid self-contradictions or biases towards the preferences of certain people (Arrow's Impossibility Theorem). Namely:

a) It should allow all preferences over fair procedures to be eligible, in the sense that if an individual prefers procedure A to B to C while another individual prefers procedure B to A to C, then the aggregating rule should consider both preferences. This condition is close to our general understanding of the term "freedom to choose". If this condition is not satisfied, then, at the limit, the aggregating rule will be like the army's rule since only one preference will be eligible for selection, i.e., the General's. And if it is the aggregating rule that decides whose preferences are eligible, then the rule itself becomes a "from without" dictator – "from without" because the rule itself is not part of the social domain of preferences.

b) If procedure A is preferred to B in the absence of C, then it should still be preferred to B in the presence of C. This condition is called the "irrelevant alternatives" and it avoids strategic manipulation and irrational behaviour such as this:
    Alma: "do you want an apple or a pear?"
    John: "An apple please"
    Alma: "I also have oranges"
    John: "Ah, in this case, I'll take a pear".

c) If all people unanimously accept a procedure as fair, then this procedure should be deemed, by the aggregating rule, as socially fair. This condition

---

[85] For a proof regarding the non-existence of an aggregating rule see Kenneth Arrow, "Social Choice and Individual Values", 1963.

states that the aggregating rule should choose the same thing that the people chose unanimously. If this condition is violated, then the rule is again a "from without" dictator, in the sense that the aggregating rule has its own mind and imposes outcomes that are not based on people's preferences.

d) A procedure should not be deemed socially fair if only one individual deems it to be so, irrespective of what everyone else thinks about it. This condition requires that no-one is a dictator. The dictator, in this case, is a dictator "from within" since his, or hers, preferences are part of the social domain of preferences.

e) If a procedure is deemed to be fairer than another procedure which in turn is deemed to be fairer than another procedure then the first procedure should also be deemed fairer than the last one. This condition is equivalent to "decisiveness" – in the sense that if it is not satisfied then the aggregating rule would not be able to decide what the outcome should be. What is wrong with indecisiveness? When the decision rule fails to reach a conclusion, policy always reverts to the status quo which may not be the preferred outcome for anyone concerned. For example, if we all want to build a park, but are unable to reach a majority decision on its size, then there is no park and we are all worse off (an outcome that is neither efficient nor fair).

The simple majority rule satisfies all the above conditions except (e). That is, under certain conditions, but not always, it fails to be decisive (the voting paradox where a majority prefers A to B, B to C and C to A). Condition (e) could be satisfied only if we violate condition (a), that is if we restrict people's freedom to choose.

∽⑨෴ൣ②

If the simple majority rule is not always decisive, does this mean that all is lost for fairness, and for democracy in general? Not exactly.

First, people who live in the same place for generations develop a culture that tends to bias their opinions towards certain definitions of fairness. In other words, culture acts as a filter that excludes many possible preferences from the social domain without angering people for not having the freedom to choose, or for not having their opinions and preferences appropriately reflected in the outcome. For example,[86] it is not an accident that most people who live in the West today would accept freedom of speech without censorship as a necessary rule for our societies. But this was not necessarily true 500 years ago in these same societies, or today in some non-Western societies. Societies with homogeneous cultures make it much easier for democracy, in general, and for fair procedures in particular, to work[87].

Second, as we mentioned earlier, we should not think of fairness as a universal rule, but rather as a contextual rule that depends on the circumstances. Universal blanket rules are generally not good because they are susceptible to "But, what if..." arguments which breed discontent and disagreement. Rules that we find fair under certain conditions, we may find unfair under some other conditions. For example, take the universal rule "thou shalt not kill". Is this a fair rule under any circumstances? No. If someone kills someone else for no reason, most people will find it extremely unfair and unjust if this person gets away unpunished. But, if the killer was minding his own business and the victim broke into his home ready to shoot him and his family, then if he was sent to prison, we will find this unfair and unjust.

Dealing with fairness on a case by case basis may lead to more agreements than disagreements, since voters evaluate one issue at the time and hence, if the choices are cleverly designed, allows us to escape the trap of Arrow's Impossibility Theorem (remember the Theorem is true when there are more than two alternatives. If there are only two alternatives, the simple majority rule satisfies all of Arrow's conditions).

A way of getting around the simple majority's indecisiveness in a multi-issue environment then is to formulate the options for collective decision-making one at a time as a "Yes" or "No" ballot (like in a referendum) [88]. Even better, formulate the answers to the questions as a "Yes" or "Come back with another proposal" ballot. The ballot could also provide voters with the opportunity to indicate what issues on the proposal they liked or disliked and hence provide

---

[86] See the November 18, 2015, "Global Support for Principle of Free Expression" by Pew Research Center where 71% of Americans, 69% of Latin Americans and 65% of Europeans say that it is very important that people can say what they want without censorship.

[87] I should emphasize here that what is homogeneous is the culture, not the racial background of the people in those societies. For example, an Irish-American who grew up in NYC is closer culturally to an Italian-American who also grew up in NYC than to an Irish-American who grew up in Idaho.

[88] Voting on one issue at a time is not problem-free either since outcomes could be path-dependent, i.e., they depend on which issue is up for vote first, second, etc. (see my book On Democracy). But it is still better than having issues decided by minorities and be also path-dependent.

the administrator of the referendum some clues on how to modify the ballot for the next round of voting.

This may sound a bit involved, i.e., having to vote several times, but in the age of the Internet it should not be much of a problem – spending a few minutes login into a website should not be more painful than loosing your health coverage, or seeing your taxes go up, or seeing your son shipped overseas to fight some unnecessary or unjust war. Or, to take a more recent real-world example, the UK could have avoided all the economic uncertainty and social anxiety around its exit from the European Union if the UK voters had the chance to specify the conditions for their vote. To ask voters whether the UK should exit the EU before the conditions of exit were in place was rather silly and undemocratic (in the sense that even the people who voted for exit would not have done so if they knew that, say, the compensation that the UK would have to pay within a year was twice the country's GDP!). As such, the only democratic thing that the UK government could do right now is to call another referendum where the present draft of the agreement is paired against the option of an exit without any agreement. And possibly a third referendum where the winner of the second round is paired against a no-exit option again.

Making decisions on a case by case basis, on the other hand, does not work very well with general policies that governments want to enact - such as the affirmative action programs that, by setting targets at the aggregate level about the promotion of certain people, leave the door wide open for these programs to be unfair at the individual level. For example, no-one would consider it fair to promote a woman whose mother is a billionaire and who attended the best schools because of her mother's donations to those schools, over, say, a black man, with the same or better skills, who grew up in the inner-city without parents and had to work two jobs to put himself through school.

Direct vs. Representative Democracy

For democracy to work as was originally intended, we need to move closer to a direct democracy model. Representative democracies are too susceptible to corruption and too removed from the wishes of the majority on most subjects.

For example, a recent study[89] found that most Americans (80%) agree that political correctness in the US today is a problem. The only group where a

---

[89] "Hidden Tribes: A Study of America's Polarized Landscape", More in Common, 2018.

majority believed the opposite accounts (the group not its majority portion) for only 8% of Americans – and yet it is their opinion that counts.

In another survey[90] on climate change, 70% of Americans believe that global warming is happening (as opposed to 14% who do not) and 57% believe that the cause of global warming is human activities (as opposed to 32% who do not). And yet, the White House is enacting policies that favour the views of these minorities on the subject! And as far as trade agreements go, the majority of Americans (56%) say that these have been good for the country, as opposed to 30% who say that they have been bad[91]. And yet again, the White House has declared war on free trade.

In most representative democracies, parties get elected not by popular vote, but rather by voters "fenced" in electoral districts of various sizes. Consequently, governing parties only rarely receive majority support. Furthermore, because political platforms are multi-issue platforms, getting majority support, by the same people, for each and everyone of the issues on their platforms is highly unlikely (remember Arrow's Impossibility Theorem applies when we have more than two issues to consider). As such, these systems fail to garner majority support on all the issues on the winning party's platform. Instead, policies are eventually enacted (not necessarily the ones on their pre-election platform) in favour of small minorities in exchange for money, or votes (see my book "*On Democracy: A Novel*") – as the previous examples on the current White House policies indicate.

It is ironic, but today's "democratic" systems in the West (except, partly, in Switzerland) seem to despise the simple majority rule, i.e., letting the majority dictate what the social outcome should be on any given subject. This is evident by their opposition to referendums and by managing to turn the word "popular" (meaning something liked by a majority) into a word with negative connotations by attaching the ending "*ism*" to it.

Nowadays, if a politician says something that has popular support, then this person is coined a "populist"! But isn't this what should happen in a democracy? No, according to the opponents of "populism" who claim that most people have no faculty for critical thinking and as such, there is no point asking them their opinion on anything. But if this is true, why would they ask them their opinion about who should represent their district? Aren't stupid

---

[90] Yale Climate Opinion Maps 2018, Aug 7, 2018, Jennifer Marlon, Peter Howe, Matto Mildenberger, Anthony Leiserowitz and Xinran Wang.
[91] "Americans are generally positive about free trade agreements, more critical of tariff increases", Pew Research Center, May, 2018.

people likely to choose a stupid person, or a sleazy deceiver, to represent them? And doesn't this render any representative democracy in the West a farcical attempt to conceal the fact that there is no democracy in the West?

Although the word "populism" has been around since the 19th Century, recently the Cambridge Dictionary declared it "the word of the year 2017", notwithstanding the fact that there is no generally accepted definition of it. According to the Cambridge Dictionary, populism is "*political ideas and activities that are intended to get the support of ordinary people by giving them what they want*" (note the near disdainful tone of the definition's ending). Well, this definition is incomplete as it does not define the words "ordinary people". If by "ordinary people" the Dictionary means a minority of people, then there is justification for its disdainful tone since this is tantamount to a *coup d'état* – hence populism, in this case, is bad. If, on the other hand, the Dictionary means a majority, then populism is good by definition and the disdainful tone is totally unwarranted.

Some people[92] think that there is a distinction between "populism" and "liberalism". But wasn't liberalism also populism 300 years ago when kings and aristocrats governed our societies? Do today's "liberals" think that the kings and aristocrats of yesteryear liked the idea of equality before the law? Or human rights?

Do I then espouse today's "populism"? No. Today's "populists" are not interested in giving a majority what it wants – if they did, they would have suggested a different system for garnering and following the wishes of the majority (a system that none of them is suggesting). Instead, they are primarily concerned with winning the elections in order to enact their own perverted, greedy, and often idiotic agendas.

"Populists" usually rise to power by sensing a popular emotion, say, people are unhappy with the present state of the economy, and putting forward "cures" that have nothing to do with improving the economy, but rather appear, at an emotional level, to do so. For example, invariably their proposals involve the time-honoured tactic of pointing the finger at one or more of the following groups: immigrants, a particular religious group, or a particular ethnic group (I should rather say Jews plus a particular ethnic group since Jews are invariably the group of choice irrespective of the country under consideration, the time frame or the issue), while at the same time wrapping themselves in the national flag: "Unemployment is high because the

---

[92] See the Munk Debate of November 2, 2018, between David Frum and Steve Bannon on the subject – a pathetic interchange where both speakers talked across purposes because they failed to define what they meant by populism.

immigrants are taking our jobs...and the Jews control everything!"; "Our national security is threatened by Islamic extremists because we allow too many Muslims into our country...and Jews!". This approach, then, combined with the fact that liberal parties nowadays tend to ignore the wishes of the majority and instead adopt top-down remedies proposed by small elites, sometimes wins the "populists" the elections.

The people who are against the simple majority rule always bring up the boogeyman of the Nazis election in Germany. But although it was true that the Germans at the time were very unhappy, having lost the war and being in the middle of an economic depression, when the Nazi party was elected in 1933, it only received 44% of the popular vote – not a majority. Had Germany had proportional representation we would have avoided WWII! Furthermore, at the time of their election, their murderous program (WWII, extermination of Jews, etc.), or Hitler's immediate actions that rendered him a dictator with the blessings of the German President, were not only unknown by the voters but were never even presented to them for voting.

A second boogeyman that opponents of direct democracy bring up is, unfortunately, an argument first stated by an otherwise brilliant man in the 19th Century – John Stuart Mill. Mill said in his book *On Liberty* (1859) that because the poor are more numerous than the rich, they could make them bear the full costs of financing public goods, or even take their money away! Although this argument could have made sense to Mill at a theoretical level, given his acceptance of utilitarianism as a model of explaining human behaviour, in reality, we have never observed such a situation - except when the poor, having had enough of being oppressed by the rich, revolt with unpredictable results since, during a revolution, the political system ceases to be democratic. If anything, what we observe in the normal course of affairs is the exact opposite! As we showed earlier with the data on wages in the United States, what we observe is that the rich, having undue influence on the political agenda, are reaping the benefits of, favorable to them, regulations.

If the "populists" of today were true populists they would seek to change the system of garnering the approval of the majority, rather than trying to deceive it by focusing their anger and unhappiness towards the wrong solutions.

As a more recent example, consider the current US President Donald Trump. Trump promised "the ordinary people" a better healthcare coverage than the one they had under President Obama and a way out of their economic misery by making America "Great Again". So, what did the "ordinary people" get when he was elected? The appointment of ex-lobbyists from the fossil fuel industry as heads of the EPA (climate change will hurt, in relative terms, "ordinary people" more than non-ordinary people), several attempts at abolishing Obama Care without any alternative plans (which would have hurt exclusively the "ordinary people"), a reduction in taxes for mainly rich individuals and large corporations (nothing ordinary about them), and tariffs on most things imported by the United States. Tariffs are taxes that Americans pay (including the "ordinary people" who, in relative terms, pay more than non-ordinary people) for consuming imported goods. The thinking here (or rather the lack of it) was that when imported goods become more expensive, this provides a stimulus to local production and hence creates jobs. But if this were a solution to the lack of local production, why not raise artificially the prices on every good and service in the US? Well, because in this case the demand will collapse and with it the US economy – producing things that no-one wants, or can afford to buy, cannot last for long! Another even stupider way of thinking about tariffs is to think of them as taxes paid by foreigners to the US administration, thus enriching the American people (this is President Trump's thinking)! And if you think that the election of Trump proves the neo-liberal point that we cannot trust people because they are stupid, think again because it was his opponent who received the majority of votes – and yet Trump was elected President!

Finally, Trump's promise of "America First" has meant pulling the US out of international agreements on things such as immigration, climate change and possibly the 1987 Intermediate-range Nuclear Forces treaty whose cancellation would lead to more spending on weapons rather than on infrastructure, education, or the poor. Since the US cannot tackle alone the issues that these agreements were meant to tackle, Trump's approach will also hurt the "ordinary people" in the long run.

So, if we need solutions to our present problems, we will need to move away from the unavoidably corrupt models of representative democracy and towards a model that is closer to direct democracy.

www.ingramcontent.com/pod-product-compliance
Lightning Source LLC
Chambersburg PA
CBHW020550220526
45463CB00006B/2253